# The
## *Joy of*
# PREACHING

# The
# *Joy of*
# PREACHING

**Fr. Rod Damico**

**Resurrection Press**
An Imprint of
**CATHOLIC BOOK PUBLISHING CO.**
Totowa • New Jersey

*Nihil Obstat:*
Msgr. John V. Wolf, STD
Censor Librorum
Columbus, Ohio

*Imprimatur*
✠ James A. Griffin, JD, JCL
Bishop of Columbus
January 3, 2001
Columbus, Ohio

First published in March, 2001 by Resurrection Press, Catholic Book Publishing Company.

Copyright © 2001 by Rod Damico

ISBN 1-878718-61-4

Library of Congress Catalog Number: 00-135229

Cover design and photo by John Murello

Printed in Canada.

1 2  3  4  5  6  7  8  9

## DEDICATION

*This first book is dedicated to those who are first in my life: Mary, my heart; Elizabeth, my sunrise; Christopher, my mountain brook; Ruth, my brilliant bolt of lightning; and Daniel, my shooting star.*

# **Contents**

# Foreword

ANOTHER book on preaching? Yes, but not *just* another book. True, Rod Damico does not replace—does not intend to replace—any of the great masters of homiletics: Buttrick and Buechner, Cox and Craddock, Waznak and Willimon. Rather, his emphasis is an uncommon monosyllable: joy. Not that other authors overlook entirely the joy of preaching: simply that joy is the thread that holds this book together.

But be forewarned, Fr. Damico's joy in preaching is not a "feel good," happy shiver that suffuses the preacher from Monday to Sunday. It goes much deeper than that, to the heart and soul of the preacher. Nor is it a joy that comes easily, automatically, simply from being a preacher. It is an emotion that is born of struggle, of effort, of suffering, of prayer.

What is uncommon, what gave *me* joy, is that *The Joy of Preaching* is not a sheerly objective presentation of a thesis. It is in large measure Damico's own story. Not an overweening, arrogant, ceaseless I, I, I. Simply that we share here one preacher's rich experience, offered with extraordinary honesty and modesty, the highly personal complemented by the communal, always the preacher in the context of the congregation. And, impressively, always aware of the God who alone can touch grace to our human words.

It is instructive to move with Damico through the preacher's itinerary. The call to preaching, his joy and his dread over speaking for God. The bouts of depression due to an inherited chemical imbalance triggered by stress. The inspiration provided by forerunners: the Hebrew prophets, Jesus, Fathers of the Church, Francis of Assisi and Francis de Sales, Dominic and Catherine of Siena. The movement from a rich Methodist ministry and the revolutionary preaching of John Wesley to an engrossing ministry within Roman Catholicism. Preparing to preach by dwelling with the Word through *lectio divina*—reading the text aloud slowly, chewing it as a cow chews its cud, awaiting God's response. Questioning the text, struggling with it, responding to it in his own life. Discussing next Sunday's readings with fifteen parishioners, to help clarify the direction of a particular homily. Having fun by brainstorming, letting the creative juices flow. Communicating through body, face, gesture as well as voice.

The joy in all this effort? "Working language into something meaningful and beautiful, the anticipation of helping to bring joy into the lives of people we care about very much." It is the joy of speaking what we love to whom we love. There is even the joy of the cross— criticism of our preaching, disinterest in the pews, the loneliness of the preacher, the inevitable sacrifices, the preacher's own inadequacies, even his failure to live what he preaches.

All this and more. And all in a pleasantly readable English that is attractive in its artlessness. No attempt at high style, alliteration, irony. What you read is . . . Rod Damico. As we New Yorkers are prone to say, "Try it, you'll like it." —Walter J. Burghardt, S.J.

# Introduction

ONE evening during my early teen years, I was asked to baby-sit for some friends from church. After they drove off to wherever it was they were going, I decided to take a little tour of the house. While passing by the master bedroom I noticed a bright yellow book on the shelf titled *The Joy of Sex*. As a young man who had recently developed quite an interest in the subject, I felt that I had come upon a treasure chest. With great enthusiasm I pulled the book off the shelf and began leafing through it. And I found some things of great interest among the pages, to be sure. But as I put the book back on the shelf, I found myself hoping that the experience itself was much more exciting than reading about it.

It is with a similar hope that I write this book. I hope that those who take it off the shelf will find it interesting. I hope that some of the pictures I have painted of the preaching life are exciting. I hope that the experiences I have related are encouraging and occasionally amusing. I hope that the practical suggestions I have offered are helpful. I hope that the joy I find in preaching has been communicated in such a way that those who have not yet experienced such joy will be in a better position to do so, and that those who have will be a bit more eager to experience it again. And yes, I really do hope that everyone who reads this little book will conclude that the experience itself is much better than reading about it—not because the book is bad, but rather because what the book speaks of is so good.

I want to make it clear that this book addresses preaching in a general way. I write as a Roman Catholic priest. But what I have to say about preaching most often applies to Christian preachers of any denomination, both clergy and lay. I rejoice that almost every Christian community recognizes that preaching is central to the ministry of the ordained. I celebrate the fact that in more recent years permanent deacons have once again taken up this ministry in the Roman Catholic Church, and often to great effect. I celebrate further that opportunities for gifted and well-trained lay preachers have increased in many of the Christian churches.

Such a small book cannot hope to cover all the various contexts for preaching.

My focus is liturgical preaching, mainly the kind of preaching that flows from biblical texts read in public worship and seeks to relate those texts to the lives of the congregation. However, much of what I have to say can be applied to preaching in any setting. For the joy of preaching is certainly not limited to the Sunday liturgy. In fact, those who have come to understand the gift and promise of preaching will always find it an occasion for joy.

# Chapter 1

# THE JOY OF BEING CALLED

"WHAT are you doing here?" This question some-times comes as a person stands before the assembly preparing to preach. It is not conveyed in a tiny whispering sound the likes of which Elijah once heard on Mt. Horeb and recognized as the voice of God. No, in this case it is the preacher's own apprehension speaking. This question of what one is doing standing in the position of preacher emerges most often as one has some clear realization of what he or she is about to do and is humbled by it. How can any human being presume to speak for God? Who is holy enough, wise enough, intelligent enough and articulate enough?

The preacher looks out on those assembled, seeing the man he forgot to visit in the hospital, the woman she spoke badly of behind her back, the child to whom he once gave a stern look for making noise in church. And again the question comes, "What am I doing here? Who am I that I should speak of God to these people, many of whom know God far better than I do?" Yet even as the question looms disturbingly before the preacher, if the preacher is truly where he or she

13

belongs and is the least bit open to it, a divine whisper of an answer will come, "You are here because I have called you." And in a moment of utter amazement, the preacher smiles and sighs, "Ah, yes. Another mystery!"

## Born in the Divine Mystery

The biblical account of the creation begins with the mystery of God's speaking. God speaks a word into nothing and something happens. This is the nature of God's word—to make something happen. God's desire is articulated and the articulation blossoms into creation. And God pronounces the fruits of his speaking good, meaning that they are in some way a genuine reflection of God's own goodness. In the beginning God spoke word after word, bringing into being a universe that expressed in some way the complexity and complementarity, the holiness and wholeness of God's own life. This always has been God's intention in speaking a creative word.

Yet those who were brought into being by his creative word did not always understand God's intentions. And often, even when they were understood, they were not accepted. As a result, life gave way to death and disintegration. So God spoke again and again, seeking to break through human resistance and to restore humankind to holiness and wholeness. At times this word was embraced and its restorative purposes were accomplished. Yet even more often people were so engulfed in the darkness of sin that they were unable to latch onto the gift of life God was offering them. Finally, unwilling to give up on the people he had made and let them sin themselves into oblivion, God spoke the ultimate saving word. God spoke himself into human life. The Word became flesh in the person of Jesus Christ and dwelt among us. The Word made visible, reaching out in compelling ways with the promise that all who accepted him would receive power to become children of God.

How the divine Word spoke himself into human life is certainly a great mystery. How does a God we cannot see or touch, a God who is without a physical body, generate speech, particularly the kind of speech that actually brings things into existence? The Word of God is born in mystery, and remains a mystery.

But perhaps just as mysterious is God's involvement of human beings in the speaking of his word. Throughout history, God has called some individuals to echo a word he has spoken to them, a word that has the power to save those for whom it is intended. That God would dignify humankind in this way, by inviting us to share in his speaking of a life-giving word, is utterly amazing. It is among the most amazing aspects of the gracious mystery of God's speaking.

We find a marvelous example of this in God's call of the prophet Jeremiah. Inviting this young man to share in the speaking of his word, God says, "Before I formed you in the womb I knew you, and before you were born I consecrated you, I appointed you a prophet to the nations" (Jer 1:5). This divine announcement came as a stunning surprise. Perhaps more than most, a young man just seeking to establish his identity in the world could see the utter ridiculousness of a human being claiming to speak for God.

In some way, this is true of all who are called to preach. It is indeed a gracious mystery since none of us is worthy of such a calling. It is also a mystery that is tinged with humor. At the burning bush God informs Moses that he has chosen this prince—turned fugitive—turned shepherd—to speak a word for him to Pharaoh. And the most hilarious thing of all is that Moses was not exactly what one would call a smooth talker! Words had never come easy for him, and the fact that he had been spending a great deal of time with sheep lately hadn't helped matters any, since sheep are not known to be the most articulate of creatures.

Yet this is part of the gracious, even hilarious mystery of the call to speak a word for God. This is God's way of showing us that he is the one who makes such things possible. God is not only the one who speaks the word in the first place, he is also the one who enables a human being to hear it and speak it to others. This is a divine gift born out of the divine mystery. So, if those who are called to preach have even the slightest sense of who they are and who is calling them, they can't help but find their being called both amazing and amusing.

## Taken Up by Divine Inspiration

If the call to preach is genuine, it is just that—a call. In other words, it is initiated by God. God catches hold of certain individuals planting within them the sense that they must speak for him. Often a sense of dread accompanies the experience of being called. "Woe is me! I am lost, for I am a man of unclean lips!" (Is 6:5). This was Isaiah's response in his initial experience of the God who was calling him to preach. As those called to preach, our immediate response to God may well be an overwhelming sense of our own limitations rather than a delightful sense of being favored with a divine visitation. Perhaps that's why one of the first things God does when calling persons to preach is to assure them he means them no harm.

This usually frees one to experience a second wave of dread as God gives the reason for this personal visit. "So come, I will send you to Pharaoh to bring my people, the Israelites, out of Egypt," God says to Moses (Ex 3:10). Who could blame Moses, who knew he was neither a good Egyptian nor a good Israelite, for responding, "Who am I that I should go to Pharaoh, and bring the Israelites out of Egypt?" (Ex 3:11). When those called to preach realize that speaking for God will set them up for public scrutiny and even ridicule, they can't help but be a bit unsettled. Thus when John was given the scroll representing the prophetic word he was to speak, while it was sweet tasting in his mouth, it turned his stomach sour (Rev 10:11). Who could blame any chosen spokespersons for getting a little sick to their stomachs when they think of the kinds of trouble they might get into for proclaiming the word of God?

Yet the vision of God that always accompanies the call to preach is so awesome and so absolutely compelling that it overrides such fears. Quite remarkably, the very thing that led to an initial sense of dread is also what unleashes the inner urge to do what God desires. This dynamic is delightfully demonstrated in the story of Isaiah's call. Recounting his encounter with God, the prophet says, "I saw the Lord sitting on a throne, high and lofty; with the hem of his robe filling the temple. Seraphs were in attendance above him . . . 'Holy, holy, holy is the LORD of hosts! The whole earth is full of his glory!' " (Is 6:3). Though initially terrified by what he saw, Isaiah was so deeply moved by the holiness of God, by the immensity of the divine majesty and glory he had been privileged to behold that when the Lord asked, "Whom shall I send? Who will go for us?" Isaiah couldn't help but respond, "Here I am, send me!" After all, once one has caught a glimpse of the glory of God without being killed by it, a little rough treatment from one's peers (or even a lot) seems a small price to pay for the possibility of catching another glimpse. In addition, the word that proceeds from this glorious God is obviously so good, holy, and true that one can hardly resist speaking it.

Though the call to preach received by some of us may not be nearly as dramatic as those we read about in scripture, God always gives this call personally. Even though it may seem to come from another person, it is really God who is speaking to the heart. It is sometimes a fuzzy awareness, to be sure, yet even a fuzzy awareness of one as great as God is compelling. And even a partial sense of the goodness and rightness of the divine word one is given to speak is infinitely more compelling than any other.

The awesome realization that God has come to us with a request to speak his wondrous word to others ignites sparks of joy and inspiration within us. The invitation to be God's partner in this work of salvation carries with it the exhilarating expectation of ongoing encounters with God. This alone provides more than enough incentive for us to swallow down our fears and take on the task.

## Taken Up with the Promise of God's Presence

The promise of God's presence is always given along with the call to preach. It is the divine trump card that renders useless even the strongest objections laid down by the preacher. Moses counters God's call to speak for him in Egypt, "I'm the only guy who ever made it onto the Most Despised Persons list for both Pharaoh and the Hebrews. There's got to be someone better suited for this than me!" And God responds, "I will be with you." Jeremiah protests God's summons to proclaim a word that will expose the sin of his people, "Lord, young people don't talk like that. I'll lose all my friends. And all the oldsters will think I've gone nuts." And God says disarmingly, "Have no fear, because I am with you." In a similar way centuries later, Jesus' disciples are shaking in their sandals lying face-down on the ground before their risen Lord who has just instructed them to take his message to all the nations. They are too frightened to speak a word of protest lest their master be reminded of their disloyalty and cowardice. And Jesus says reassuringly, "Know that I am with you always."

This promise of God's presence always comes along with the call to preach because it is only with the constant presence of God that such work can be accomplished. The life of a preacher can be very lonely at times. The companionship of one who understands what we are doing and supports us completely in the doing of it is essential. Speaking a word that challenges people to change, to see and do things differently, can create a sense of isolation that could be totally overwhelming at times without a companion who understands and supports us in our work as preachers. For this reason, it is important that those who preach do whatever is necessary to remain mindful of the promised presence of God. Though it may not always be felt, because God has promised it, God's presence is something we can always count on.

The promise of God's presence means that there is always one with us who:

- Understands exactly what we are talking about because he gave us the word in the first place
- Knows just how important what we are doing really is because he's the one who called us to it
- Appreciates our sense of delight in the work of preaching because he is the one who inspires us to do delightful things
- Is genuinely aware of just how hard the preaching life is for us at times because he remains at our side through times of struggle, doubt, discouragement, and fatigue

More than any other, he realizes the toll preaching takes on us because he knew us thoroughly before we were conceived in the womb and understood, even then, exactly what being a preacher would cost us.

In addition to such personal support, the constant companionship of God also carries with it the assurance of divine assistance with the actual work to be done. Those of us who have been preaching awhile know what it's like to open the scripture, to study, pray, and listen as intently as we can for the word God wants us to preach and, much to our distress, hear absolutely nothing. We know what it's like to look out on a crowd of people as we preach our hearts out only to see blank faces, a frown, an occasional yawn, and children drawing pictures while chewing on Cheerios. Yet, we also know what it's like to wake up, after several days of struggle and fervent prayer, with a wonderful new idea of how to approach our preaching that fills us with excitement. We know what it's like to read a scripture passage for the hundredth time when suddenly the divine word bursts forth from the text like Jack finally busting out of his box. And we know what it's like to have someone, who seemed to be sleeping through the whole of our preaching, come up to us afterwards and say with genuine enthusiasm that our message moved him deeply.

In the quiet moments when we reflect on all these things, we begin to have more than a suspicion that our unseen companion has been doing a little more than sightseeing. We come to recognize the insight that finally comes, the word that suddenly emerges, and the opening of hearts and minds to what we have to say as gifts of God. More than just holding our hands, the God who calls us to preach is present with us to help us.

Of course, all this is not to say that we do not need the companionship of others in the preaching life. We do. Because we are human and are made to be in relationship with other human beings, we often need a skin-clad presence to support and help us in our lives as preachers. And the importance of this can only be diminished to our own diminishment. But in the long run, the knowledge that God is always with us is what matters most. There is no greater joy in the preaching life than to realize that embracing the call to preach has placed us in a special relationship with the One who brought everything into existence through the speaking of a word, who sustains everything in being by his life-giving presence, and who loves all he has made, including us, with the greatest of all loves.

## Taken Up for the Sake of God's People

As those of us who are called to preach journey with God, we can't help but develop a deep caring for God's people. This word we preach is born out of love. It is an expression of God's concern for his people. To those who hear it, it is God's gracious appeal to come to him and let him bring them into the full and eternal life of his kingdom. Perhaps the most obvious thing that can be said about preaching, then, is that it is taken up for the sake of God's people.

In the eighth chapter of Acts, we are told about a man from Ethiopia, one of the queen's officials who had come to Jerusalem to worship. It is not clear whether this man was a convert to Judaism or simply one who was attracted to it. But one thing is clear. He still hadn't found what he was looking for. The Ethiopian was reading from the scroll of Isaiah during his ride back home when Philip, a Spirit-driven preacher if there ever was one, caught up with him and asked if he understood what he was reading. The response was simple and terribly suggestive. "How can I, unless someone instructs me?" So Philip did just that. Beginning with the scripture passage the Ethiopian was reading, he proclaimed the good news of Christ to him. As the story goes, the inquirer was so moved by this bit of impromptu preaching that he asked to be baptized right on the spot!

If people are going to come to faith in Christ, then they must be told about him in some compelling way. In Paul's wonderful rhetorical fashion, he echoes this point made so dramatically in the story of the Ethiopian official: "But how are they to call on one in whom they have not believed? And how are they to believe in one of whom they have not heard? And how are they to hear without someone to proclaim him?" (Rom 10:14). In our own day this basic truth has found powerful expression in the "Decree on the Ministry and Life of Priests" from the Second Vatican Council. Speaking of the necessity of preaching for the life of faith and for salvation, the document states:

"The people of God are first gathered together by the word of the living God, which they have a right to seek from the mouth of priests. No one can be saved except by first having believed. Priests, therefore, have for their first responsibility the proclaiming of God's gospel to all . . . Thus the saving word gives birth to faith in the hearts of non-believers and nurtures it in the hearts of believers. Faith, then, is what begins and increases the community of believers." (II.1.4)

Priests and all others, who are called to the work of preaching, must never lose sight of the purpose behind what they do. While it may be exciting to be called to speak on behalf of God; while it may be an exhilarating exercising of one's gifts; and while it may indeed draw one more deeply into a relationship with God, the primary reason for the call to preach is to benefit God's people. Because of this, preachers will always find their greatest joy in discovering that the word they have proclaimed has helped someone come to faith or grow in faith. This, most of all, is what causes preachers to go on their way rejoicing.

## A Preacher's Experience

The joy of being called to preach is no abstract reality. It is something truly experienced in the life of the preacher. And because each preacher is unique, each one will experience it a little differently. In my own life, the call to preach was certainly born in mystery. I have always been a very shy and retiring type. Yet, as part of a deep experience of God's presence during the summer of my senior year in high school, God planted within me a desire to speak of him to others. And though the level of intensity has varied at times, the desire has never left.

Now, some thirty years later, the mystery of one such as me being called to preach has expanded quite mysteriously. I am still shy and reclusive in nature. Only now, in addition, I have suffered through many bouts of depression, due to a chemical imbalance that is triggered by stress. And God has called me to a position that requires me to be involved in public speaking almost every day! Add to this the unusual circumstance of my being the only married priest in our diocese and we come up with the following formula: A married priest, who prefers to melt into the background unnoticed and is inclined to depression triggered by stress, has been called by God to stand before groups of people and preach almost daily. If that's not a mystery, then nothing is! In light of this, all one can conclude is that God must have a great sense of humor. And his genius must be beyond comprehension to make it all work.

The desire to preach was given in a moment when I was so overwhelmed by a sense of the greatness of God, by God's infinite goodness and love, that though I would never have chosen the preaching life myself, the thought of refusing God's call never even crossed my mind.

Yet this does not mean that the preaching life has been easy for me. At times it has taken a great toll. On occasion I have tried to argue like Moses, Jeremiah, and others that I am not suited for such work. However, this has been no more effective for me than it was for them. In fact, when I think of abandoning such work because it is too draining or too hard, I find myself feeling much like Jeremiah who once exclaimed, "If I say, 'I will not mention him, or speak any more in his name,' then within me there is something like a burning fire shut up in my bones; I am weary with holding it in, and I cannot" (Jer 20:9).

How can I not speak of the God who has been my constant companion these many years? While my family and close friends know the peaks and valleys of my life's journey, only God knows the deepest, most intimate aspects of my personal odyssey. Only God knows the immensity of joy that overwhelms me at times when I am with my wife and children. God alone knows how hard it is for me at times to even lift one foot and place it in front of the other. God alone knows the quickening of spirit I experience when I am able to speak a word that actually helps someone who is in a difficult situation. And God alone knows how wonderfully the faint glowing embers of faith are fanned into white hot flames within me through the faithful witness often made by the sick and dying when I come to bring them a word of comfort.

How can I not speak of this God whose presence makes it possible for me to speak the word he has placed within my heart? So often I have struggled all week with a word that needs to be preached. Yet I cannot find the story or image that will make it possible for people to see what this word has to do with them. The night before I absolutely must put something together I wrack my brain and pray myself to sleep. And in the morning the story or image is there. The flow of the homily runs through my mind so clearly that I am absolutely awestruck. I realize that the Lord has been busy while I have been sleeping, giving a little divine assistance to whatever gifts of creativity I possess.

Occasionally I have come to the time of preaching feeling so dead inside that it is all I can do to keep breathing. Yet, as I stand before the people, I am suddenly filled with an energy and joy that astounds me. There are times when I am not quite sure what the word is that God wants me to speak at a daily Mass or at one of our high school Masses, and I am amazed by the words that flow out of my mouth as I stand before the people. They are more beautiful and more perfectly integrated than are some of my most finely crafted homilies. And I am happily reminded of his promise to give words to those who are willing to risk making a fool of themselves.

And the most amazing thing of all is that while I am being helped by God to speak his word, God's people are being helped by the words I speak. At times people will tell me that their family discussed my homily on the way home from church and decided to do some things differently as a result. Often parishioners will request a copy of a particular homily to send to friends or relatives because they think it might help them. I was stunned recently when a man told me that my preaching had meant so much to him that he thought I should put each week's homily on the parish web page! To discover that what I put so much time and effort into really makes a difference for the people God has called me to serve is truly one of my greatest joys.

# Chapter 2

# THE JOY OF JOINING A GREAT COMPANY OF WITNESSES

DURING a recent vacation to the state of New York our family spent a day at the Baseball Hall of Fame in Cooperstown. Baseball has always occupied a significant place in our family life. We are all both players and fans. So this shrine to the "national pastime," was an exciting place to visit. We were fascinated by stories of the game's great pioneers, like Harry Wright, who organized, managed and played center field for baseball's first professional team, the 1869 Cincinnati Red Stockings and A.G. Spalding, who helped organize the National league in 1876 while pitching his team to forty-seven victories that year. We moved on to exhibitions featuring baseball giants from the early days of the twentieth century, when players dressed and played the game much differently than they do now— Walter Johnson, Christy Matthewson, Cy Young, Nap Lajoie, Ty Cobb, to name only a few.

We found ourselves in much more familiar territory when we got to the displays featuring those players who, through their extraordinary talent and force of personality, brought the game to national prominence in the 1920s and 1930s. Players like Babe Ruth, Lou Gehrig, Dizzy Dean and Lefty Gomez established baseball as part of the fabric of life in the United States. Moving on, we were intrigued by the story of those women who answered the call to become professional ball players and carry on the saga of the sandlots during the Second World War. From there the photo litany of former stars continued, featuring such heroes as Bob Feller, Joe DiMaggio, Jackie Robinson, Ted Williams, Willie Mays, Mickey Mantle, Sandy Koufax, Johnny Bench, and Nolan Ryan. Each one of these "Hall of Famers" accomplished something in their careers that left a lasting impression.

Finally we came to that section of the museum dedicated to the stars of the present day. Though not yet elected to the Hall of Fame, these current standouts are the ones who have touched young fans most significantly. In fact, I noticed even very young children, pulling parents over to a display featuring Mark McGwire or Randy Johnson and telling them all about these current superstars of the grand old game.

This time of connecting with the great tradition of baseball had quite an impact on us. It led to conversations about how strange the early ball players looked, and how difficult it must have been to play the game without the kinds of gloves and other protective equipment used today. We marveled at the dedication of these pioneers, who devoted themselves to a game that must have seemed quite silly to many. And when we stopped later on to play a little baseball ourselves, we had fun imitating some of baseball's greats, demonstrating how "The Babe" stepped up to the plate, how Willie Mays made those exciting "Basket Catches," how Juan Marichal lifted his leg so high before he fired the ball plate-ward. This plunge into baseball's grand tradition had obviously filled us with a fresh enthusiasm for the game.

When we arrived back home, we noticed that our visit to Cooperstown definitely had an impact on the way we played the game. My wife and I took the field with a little more energy and determination as we rejoined our respective slow pitch softball teams. My sons couldn't wait to rejoin their teams and get back on the field themselves. As I watched them play, I was able to see little things they were doing that reminded me of some of the great gurus from the past. But the most obvious imitating was of the stars of today. And when their gaze met mine, we smiled the knowing smile of those who have come to see that they are part of something grand.

I think it is not too far a stretch to say that preachers will experience something similar when they take the time to connect with the grand tradition of which we are a part. As we move through the pages of the Old Testament and take in the stories of the great pioneers of preaching we can't help but be inspired by their courage and their powerful proclamations. When we journey with Jesus through the Gospels, we encounter the heart and soul of all Christian preaching. Remembering the preaching of the apostles connects us in an exciting way with the heroic dedication of those who gave their all to establish the Church throughout the world. Learning about those who carried on this great tradition of preaching over the centuries provides us with a sense of being part of something immensely rich and of the utmost significance for human life. And acquainting ourselves with the great preachers of the present helps us to develop the approaches, techniques, and enthusiasm necessary for preaching effectively in the world of today.

## Inspired by the Forerunners

Most of us involved in the ministry of preaching have times when we feel like oddballs. It's bound to happen, since there are relatively few of us. Also, we are often called to preach a message that challenges popular beliefs and practices. And even when we are given a consoling or encouraging word to speak, it is not always based on anything immediately apparent to the hearers. It comes instead as a gift of God's mysteriously active presence, making us something of a mystery to most. At such times there is no better place to turn than to the Old Testament prophets, the pioneers and forerunners of all Christian preachers. Their courage in proclaiming a word of truth that often set them at odds with their people is truly uplifting.

Anyone who has ever felt a bit nervous venturing into the pulpit to speak a word that calls people to repentance and conversion can't help but be inspired by revisiting the story of Nathan's confrontation with King David in the twelfth chapter of Second Samuel. To save himself from public scandal over his adulterous affair with Bathsheba, David had caused the death of an honorable man. It's hard to imagine the moxie it must have taken for Nathan to declare his divinely revealed knowledge of David's misdeeds. In comparison it makes most of our preaching seem like a stroll in the park.

Those preachers who have spoken courageously like Nathan and are feeling disheartened by a cool response would do well to review the preaching career of the prophet Jeremiah. If ever there was a preacher disheartened by the response of his people to the message he proclaimed, it was Jeremiah. We can't help but be moved by his intensity as he speaks of being mocked, attacked, and plotted against for speaking God's word. And this was the response of those who had been his friends! Jeremiah was so devastated that he even cursed the day he was born. Yet somehow he was able to summon the strength necessary to keep on preaching throughout his life, becoming one of the greatest forerunners of those who preach the Gospel.

A quick reviewing of his story can lift up the heart of even the most downtrodden preacher with the knowledge that it is possible to persevere. Perhaps we can even laugh a little at ourselves, realizing that if we haven't been thrown down into the bottom of a muddy cistern and left to die because of our preaching, then we can consider ourselves lucky!

Actually, preachers struggling with almost any aspect of the preaching life can find inspiration somewhere among the Old Testament prophets. Those struggling with serious theological questions will get a charge out of Habakkuk, who was so disturbed by the old conundrum of why good people suffer and evil people prosper that he planted himself on a watchtower and refused to come down until God gave him an answer. Those who are a bit more brazen will be buoyed up by the prophet Amos, whose very first sermon began, "The Lord roars from Zion"; and who had the nerve to call some of the high-class women of his day the "cows of Bashan"!

Those with a penchant for symbolic expression will be stimulated by Hosea, who married a harlot as a way of symbolizing that God's people had prostituted themselves religiously; and Isaiah, who gave his children such meaning-laden names as "A remnant shall return," and "The spoil speeds, the prey hastens." Those more inclined to the visionary will be energized by Ezekiel, while those of a more apocalyptic bent will be delighted by Daniel. Among the forerunners of new covenant preachers there is to be found more than enough to fuel the fervor of us all. So it is good to return to them often.

## Rooted in Jesus

Of course, the Christian life is rooted in Jesus. This means that when it comes to preaching, as with all other aspects of the Christian life, it is best to begin with him. In Jesus we discover the essential purpose and methodology of preaching. In him we find the resources that make the preaching life possible.

As the incarnate Word, Jesus was himself the fulfillment of all that was foretold by the prophets. In his preaching he announced this fulfillment. In word and deed he proclaimed that the door to participation in God's kingdom was now being opened for all. And he invited people to the kind of conversion of life that would make this participation possible. Jesus' preaching, then, was a matter of proclamation and invitation.

Jesus employed a very simple, but also very comprehensive, methodology in the making of this proclamation and invitation. In his preaching, he often referred to the scriptures, interpreting them in a way that shed light on God's continuing presence in him. He spoke simply, in the common language of the people. But he used various forms of speech, depending on the audience, the circumstances, and the particular message he wanted to convey. Though perhaps he is best known for his parables, Jesus also made good use of declarative and discursive speech. Or to put it another way, to the hardhearted, he presented stories and images that were intended to break through their emotional barriers; to the hardheaded, he made clear statements of truth that were intended to shatter their intellectual illusions; and to the confused, he offered simple explanations of what God was doing and why.

Perhaps most importantly, what Jesus said was always supported in some way by what he did. His announcement of the in-breaking of the reign of God was accompanied by physical healings and the casting out of demons. His proclamation of God's special concern for the poor was given visible expression in the personal attention and assistance he gave to the poor. His declaration of God's unconditional love for all people was supported by his eating and drinking both with respected citizens and with social outcasts. His promise of God's forgiveness for all who truly repented was reflected in his gracious reception of notorious sinners who came to him seeking mercy. For Jesus, it was not a matter of preaching the word and doing good deeds. Rather, speech and action together constituted his preaching.

In addition to showing us what we are to preach and how we are to preach it, Jesus also revealed to us the underlying means of inspiration and support necessary for the preaching life. In a statement summarizing the early days of Jesus' ministry, Luke says, "Many crowds would gather to hear him and to be cured of their diseases. But he would withdraw to deserted places and pray" (Lk 5:15b-16). At another time Jesus told his disciples a parable about the need to "pray always and not to lose heart" (Lk 18:1). More extended times of private prayer, in which he communed deeply with his heavenly Father, along with frequent spontaneous turnings to God during the course of his busy days, provided Jesus with the knowledge of what needed to be preached, as well as the strength and motivation needed to keep on preaching.

In summary, then, if our preaching is to be rooted in the preaching of Jesus, it will proclaim the wonderful gift of salvation offered to all people in him and invite the kind of conversion of life necessary to embrace it. It will refer frequently to the scriptures, showing how the inspired word speaks to the present situation. It will utilize a rich variety of speech forms intended to break through to people of different orientations and circumstances. It will constantly integrate speech and action. It will rely on frequent and sometimes extended periods of turning to God for the inspiration to know what to preach and to receive the resources necessary to sustain us in the preaching life.

Rooting our preaching in the preaching of Jesus is a special way of participating in the paschal mystery. As Jesus did, in our preaching we will have to die to self in some way for the sake of others. We will have to set aside our personal desires and inclinations. The less studious among us will have to devote time to studying the scriptures. The more intellectual among us will have to learn to speak simply. The more mystically oriented will have to make concrete applications, while the more practically oriented will have to speak of mysterious things. The more passive will have to back their speaking up with some kind of corresponding action, while the more active will have to slow down long enough to develop preaching material that will impart a sense of why such action is necessary.

When we make such sacrifices for the sake of the people, our preaching becomes fruitful. In our own dying to self, we make it possible for others to come to life. In the process, we come to share ever more fully in the dying and rising of Jesus. We discover that when our preaching is rooted in Jesus, in addition to helping others, we ourselves are set on the road to salvation. So it is our glory, our salvation, and our great joy to preach as Jesus did.

## Built on the Foundation of the Apostles

The first to preach as Jesus did were the apostles. Their purpose was not to proclaim what God was doing through them, but rather what God had done and was continuing to do through Jesus. They were to be his witnesses. They were to invite people to a conversion of life that began with the embracing of Jesus as their savior, who not only opened for them the doorway into the kingdom but also revealed to them the path of life that leads to it.

While modeling their preaching after the preaching of Jesus, the apostles were faced with a three-fold challenge: to reach out to those who had yet to believe in Jesus in a way that invited their conversion; to help those who had already believed understand and embrace it ever more fully; and to set straight those who, in some way, had strayed from the gospel. While it is sometimes suggested that the apostles devoted themselves primarily to the more kerygmatic type of preaching, that is, preaching which sought to convert, their prominence in the life of the Church certainly necessitated their involvement with didactic (teaching) and prophetic (reforming) types of preaching as well. And, all three types of preaching, in various combinations and proportions, have been present in the preaching of the Church ever since.

In addition to the foundational character of their preaching, what makes the apostles so important for those who take up the preaching life is the boldness with which they preached. Unfortunately, we do not have any detailed records of the preaching careers of the apostles. However, it is the strong testimony of tradition that the kind of boldness and dedication that typified the preaching ministries of Peter and Paul as described in the Book of Acts, was actually typical of all the apostles.

While in many ways the preaching life of the apostles remains shrouded in mystery, the fact that the Church grew as it did bears witness to their dedication and to the effectiveness of their preaching. Especially in those moments when we begin to feel a bit overwhelmed in our own preaching ministries, it is good to remember the apostles. With the Lord's help they were able to give themselves fully to their vocation as preachers of the Gospel. And the fact that we are involved in the work of preaching now is testimony to the enduring significance of their faithfulness. Remembering that our own preaching ministry is built on the foundation of the apostles and is in a real sense a continuation of what they began can renew our enthusiasm. It can restore the smiles to our faces and fill our hearts with joy.

## Nurtured by the Great Preachers of the Past

A great company of preachers has been raised up from the strong foundation provided by the apostles. Outstanding preachers have blessed every generation of the Church's history. And many continue to be remembered. Though these preachers vary greatly in terms of personality, style, situation in life, and historical context, we have something to learn from all of them. Usually the most valuable lessons do not have to do with rhetorical style, biblical interpretation, or sermon construction. Rhetorical styles are constantly changing, as are patterns of speech and cultural context. Add to this the rapid development of the electronic media and it should be pretty obvious that the greatest sermons of even a few generations past, preached verbatim and in a similar style, would not leave today's congregations standing with lights glowing, begging for more!

Certainly there are many things to be learned from the great preachers of the past with regards to the method and content of preaching. Perhaps in a particular collection of sermons we will find an interesting homiletical movement, a stunning phrase, an illuminating interpretation of scripture, a useful image or a fascinating story. Often of much greater significance are the life stories of the preachers themselves. As we become familiar with these life stories we discover how they came to take up the preaching life and what sustained them in it. We come to see what kind of impact they had on the people of their day and the effect this had on their own personal lives.

As we become familiar with the lives of great preachers from past generations we will find much that will nurture us in the preaching life today. Among them we can all find heroes who challenge us, enliven us, and with whom we can relate in some personal way. Lay preachers may look to someone like Origen, a layman of the third century who emerged as the first great preacher in the early Church. His rhetorical style and his method of scripture interpretation captivated thousands and had a profound impact on the development of liturgical preaching. Laypersons discouraged by their lack of significant preaching opportunities can look to Origen for a rekindling of hopeful enthusiasm.

Augustine is a good mentor whose life and preaching can provide much nourishment for those who are profoundly moved by their own life experience to call others to ongoing conversion and a fuller embracing of the great truths of our faith. Those free spirits among us, who are more inclined to spontaneity and mobility, can find an exciting model in Francis of Assisi, while those inclined to be more stable and pastoral have much to gain from getting to know Francis de Sales. Some who are driven by a passionate concern for advancing the truth of the Gospel in ways that expose the falsehoods many people have chosen to live by can receive much needed affirmation from Dominic, who founded the Order of Preachers for just this purpose. Women seeking inspiration for their preaching ministry may look to Catherine of Siena, a woman of the fourteenth century. Her fiery preaching, complemented by tireless service to others and deep experiences of prayer, brought about remarkable transformations in people's lives.

Preachers wanting to set hearts aflame for the living Christ will find strong support in the person of George Whitefield, that preacher of the Great Awakening, who was so skilled at moving the hearts of his hearers that it is said he could make people weep just by the way he pronounced "Mesopotamia." Those who are called to preach in new and unusual settings can receive encouragement from John Wesley, who accepted the challenge to break with established custom and go outside the empty Anglican churches of the eighteenth century to preach to thousands in the fields of the English countryside. Preachers who are filled with compassion for the plight of the poor will be invigorated by the preaching of Mother Teresa and Oscar Romero, whose words and actions together formed a marvelously compelling message.

If preachers are going to maintain their enthusiasm and continue to grow in the exercising of this ministry, it is very helpful to devote some time to learning about great preachers of the past. In addition to being uplifted by the knowledge that the ministry of preaching has been carried on effectively by followers of Jesus for over twenty centuries now, each one of us will find ourselves connecting in special ways with some of these preachers. They will become for us mentors and companions, whose examples we seek to imitate and whose heavenly intercessions we rely on to sustain us in our work. In being thus nurtured by the great preachers of the past we encounter another source of joy in the preaching life.

## Formed by the Preachers of the Present

While we receive much from the great preachers of the past in terms of inspiration, encouragement, purpose and direction, undoubtedly it is the preachers of the present that have the greatest influence on our actual preaching. Computers, satellites, and other new communications technologies have increased the accessibility of people and information in a way unknown to previous generations. Developments in the biological sciences have changed the way we understand and relate to the world around us. And certainly the evolution of recreation and entertainment has had a profound impact on people's expectations and desires. While much about human life remains the same, the present time in human history is truly unique. And since effective communication is so obviously related to life context, it only stands to reason that those who have learned to preach effectively in our contemporary context will be of the greatest help in the development of our own preaching manners and methods.

While back at the turn of the fifth century John the Golden Mouthed (Chrysostom) may have been able to hold congregations spellbound for long periods of time with his classic oratorical skills, using the same methods today, one would more likely be known as Leaden Mouthed. The sweeping scope of classical rhetoric does not work nearly so well when one is preaching to people who are going to have to dash off to a child's ball game in a half-hour, who can spend an evening "surfing the net" for interesting bits of information, and who have beepers and cell phones in their pockets that may occasionally require their attention during the homily. If we are looking for an interesting interpretation of a passage of scripture, a bit of solid theology to reflect upon, a striking application of the Word of God to everyday life, or simply the inspiration to be gained from connecting with one of the great preachers of the past, then turning to Chrysostom is helpful. However, if we want to learn something about preaching an engaging homily now, we will be better served by turning to one of the great preachers of today.

Besides, we learn best from what we experience. When it's time for children to learn to tie their shoes, parents do not set them down with a book that describes the history and methods of shoe tying. Nor do they simply tell them how it's done. Instead, they show them how it's done. So it is with preaching. We learn it by watching those who know how to do it and at times even inviting them to help us improve our preaching.

Anyone serious about developing as a preacher should make it a point to actually experience good preaching from time to time. Preaching is an event that cannot be fully captured in print or even on tape. It is something that is only experienced fully when it is happening. In the experiencing of it we are impacted on a variety of levels, some conscious and some unconscious. We begin to develop an awareness of what makes for good preaching even before we begin to think about it. Simply put, our fundamental formation as preachers does not begin in a book or in the classroom. It begins in the pew.

And where is such excellent preaching to be found? Actually, great preaching is quite accessible to all of us. We will often experience wonderful preaching at Church conferences and parish missions. Another way to experience outstanding preaching is to participate in summer programs or seminary courses designed to develop the skills of those who are already involved in preaching ministries. The additional benefit of this particular setting is that time is actually taken to discuss what made the preaching good. Of course, in addition to these more "exotic" settings, most of us have excellent preaching going on right in our own back yards. In almost any geographic area there will be at least a few men and women who have acquired the reputation of being outstanding preachers.

Taking the time necessary to experience the preaching of contemporary pulpit masters will not only make us better preachers but also bring a greater depth of joy to the preaching life. It's like aspiring young ball players watching a game well played by some of the stars of the game. It makes them want to get out and play well themselves. In the same way, when we experience good preaching, we are reminded of why we got excited about preaching in the first place. We are filled with a new resolve to improve our own preaching. And the challenge of preparing and preaching a great homily becomes a glorious adventure once again.

## A Preacher's Experience

As the love of baseball is born in the hearts of ball players by watching others who love the game play it well, so the love of preaching was born in me when, as a young man, I experienced great preaching for the first time. The summer before my senior year in high school I had a conversion experience and started going to church. Since I had no real church background, but had suddenly become intensely interested in religion, a good friend invited me to attend a nearby Methodist church with him. Thankfully, the church had an excellent preacher. The fact that I remember Dr. Thomas Luke's name some thirty years later says something significant about the impact he had on my life. I was often moved deeply by what he had to say about faith in Christ and what it had to do with our lives. As I observed the attentiveness of others during his sermons, I realized that they were being impacted in a similar way. This experience of good preaching, coupled with my newly born enthusiasm for the faith, filled me with a great desire to preach. I had received "the call" and was eager to respond.

As I went off to college to begin my preparation for the Methodist ministry and the preaching life, I had a very simplistic view of the task of preaching. I saw learning to preach as being very similar to learning to tie shoes. In other words, one became a good preacher by watching someone who was already good at it. Then you simply kept trying to do what that preacher did until you finally got quite good at it yourself. While I realized that future ministers of the Gospel had to learn about scripture, theology, and church history for some reason, when it came to preaching, I believed that you either had the gift or you didn't and that was that.

Almost unavoidably over the years I learned that that was not that! Through my college and seminary years I had the opportunity to experience many different preachers, discovering that there was definitely more than one way to preach effectively. I began to realize that, rather than simply copying the style of another, it was important to recognize one's own gifts and to use them well.

During my days at Baldwin-Wallace College I was awed by the great intensity with which my Old Testament professor, John Trever, read the words of the prophets. Suddenly the prophets became people living real lives, saying outrageous things, and getting themselves into all kinds of trouble for it. It was in his classroom that my great interest in the prophets as preachers came to life.

During my days at Yale Divinity School, I was so stirred by professor Roland Bainton's dramatic portrayal of Martin Luther preaching his famous Christmas sermons that I began to collect (and occasionally even read) the sermons and homilies of significant figures in the church's history along with their biographies. As one preparing for the Methodist ministry I began to take a special interest in the life and preaching of John Wesley. Though I didn't realize it at the time, my growing connection with the larger historic community of preachers was to pay rich dividends in years to come.

In my early days as a Methodist minister I suffered a great deal of anticipatory anxiety with regards to preaching. I was so concerned about not being adequately prepared that I usually completed a manuscript for the next Sunday's sermon by Tuesday afternoon! Then I would go over it again and again until it was indelibly etched in my memory. And still I was nervous when Sunday morning came around. During those days I found it helpful to remember the kinds of preaching situations that the apostles faced on a regular basis. They often spoke boldly before disrespectful or even hostile crowds, and risked their very lives to preach the Gospel. After thinking of Paul preaching at the Areopagus, I would say to myself, "And you're nervous about getting up and preaching to this little gathering of people who all love you?" The members of the congregation must have wondered at times why I was shaking my head and smiling when I stepped into the pulpit.

After a few years of preaching in the same church week after week, I wasn't nearly as nervous about being in the pulpit, but I did get discouraged at times. I worked hard preparing my sermons. And I put my whole heart and soul into the preaching of them. Yet, when I thought of our church community and the lives of many of its members, it seemed to me that nothing much had changed. My frequent challenges toward ongoing conversion and growth had, for the most part, gone unheeded. I sometimes felt like giving up. At such times the stories of the prophets often came to the rescue.

I would come across a text like 1 Kings 19:1-18. Elijah had fled to the desert. His work as a prophet had finally become too much for him. But after letting the prophet run for forty days and forty nights God spoke to him. "Get back to work! Yes, I know most people haven't listened to you. Believe me, they're going to be the worse off for it. But some have listened. And they need you." So Elijah got back to work.

Remembering his story helped me get back to work too. And when I thought about it, I realized that my preaching really did make a difference to some. This was usually enough to chase away the clouds of discouragement and allow me to find joy in the ministry of preaching once again.

Making such connections with preachers of the past has truly been a lifeline for me over the years. Perhaps one of the most interesting experiences of this occurred several years after my conversion to Roman Catholicism. Among other things I had now moved from "sermons" to "homilies." But depression had again taken a strong hold on me. At times the darkness was so thick I could not see the fire of faith or the light of truth glowing within me. I began to feel badly about preaching the Gospel to others while I was so out of touch with the God of life myself. During a counseling session with a parishioner, who had come to talk with me about her own depression and the guilt she was feeling about no longer being enthusiastic in the practice of her faith, quite unexpectedly I found myself relating to her the story of John Wesley.

I told her of Wesley's disastrous experience as an Anglican missionary in Georgia. The end result was that, to save his skin, he had to abandon his work and flee to his native England. The young priest was humiliated because of the foolish things he had done and by his failure to win converts and turn the hearts of lukewarm Christians more fully to the Lord. Not surprisingly, during the long ship ride home, Wesley sunk into a terrible depression. He began to feel that he could no longer preach because he had lost the strong sense of faith that had been his motivation. Thankfully, Wesley confided this to a Moravian minister who happened to be on board. With the kind of gentle wisdom for which the Moravians were famous, he advised Wesley "to preach faith until he had it." In other words, he encouraged him to preach the faith he knew but no longer felt until he felt it once again. Wesley took this advice to heart and put it into practice with the result that eventually he did come to feel the fires of faith burning within him once again. In fact, they began to burn with such fervency that he ignited a religious revolution in England that set thousands on fire for the Lord.

My Catholic parishioner was moved by this story of the founder of Methodism. But the truth is that I was moved more. After this, as I struggled with preaching through my own depression, I remembered Wesley often. His story helped to sustain me as a preacher until I began to feel alive again. When I thought of him I had a deep sense of comfort and even joy in sharing such a special connection with this great Christian witness.

I truly have been inspired and nurtured by many of the great preachers of the past. Yet, the most fundamental influence has been the Lord Jesus himself, whom I seek to follow in all things. Like Jesus, I try to preach simply, in the language of the people. I try to use stories and images that will help people see how their daily life is related to God. I try to reflect God's special concern for the poor, as well as God's great compassion for all who suffer. In as many ways as I can, I challenge people to follow Jesus in dying to self in order to live fully for God and God's people.

In addition to following the Lord's lead, I have been influenced most in the development of my own preaching style by the preaching I have experienced firsthand over the years. I have participated in many conferences and community ecumenical events that featured excellent preachers, who tell engaging stories, often with a personal dimension; who make clear connections between the scripture and the common life of the assembly; who put it all together in a way that focuses on a single clear message; and whose presentation has some passion to it. Since this is the kind of preaching that has stirred me the most, this is what I try to do in my own preaching.

In terms of reflecting a bit more deeply on various aspects of the preaching life, I have found it helpful to work an occasional book or article on preaching into my reading schedule. Books by Frederick Buechner and Thomas Troeger have always managed to get my creative juices flowing. Fred Craddock and Robert Waznak have helped me refine the process of creating a homily that flows from the biblical text in a way that is both faithful to the text and engages the life of the people. Thomas Long and Mary Catherine Hilkert have stimulated my thoughts on the nature and function of preaching. The writings of Walter Burghardt and Walter Brueggemann have made me more sensitive to the social dimensions of preaching. And the printed homilies of Barbara Brown Taylor and John Paul II have often challenged me to work a bit harder on my own. These and many others have contributed to my understanding and practice of preaching in ways that have enriched me greatly. And what joy there is in being, in some small way, part of this great company of witnesses!

# Chapter 3

# THE JOY OF DWELLING
# WITH THE WORD

THE eighth chapter of the Book of Nehemiah recounts a most remarkable event. To celebrate the restoration of Jerusalem and its temple following the exile, all the Jews who had returned to rebuild their country came to the holy city for a great assembly. Ezra, the scribe, took his place on a wooden platform made especially for the occasion. He opened the Torah scroll in the sight of all the people. As he opened it, everyone rose in honor of God's holy word. Filled with joy, Ezra blessed the Lord. And with hands raised high, the people responded with their own hearty "Amen." Then in reverence, they prostrated themselves before the Lord. Following this glorious beginning to their re-gathering as a holy people, Ezra read the Torah to them for several hours. He interpreted the text as he went along, so that all could understand what had been read.

As Ezra read and explained the meaning of God's word the people were moved to tears. And being moved himself by this marvelous sight, Ezra spoke words of encouragement. He told his people that this was not a day to be saddened by what they had lost over the years. Instead, it was a day to rejoice in the wonderful gift they were now receiving. So the people went home rejoicing. They celebrated with the choicest food and drink, sharing generously with those who had none. All were filled with joy because they had heard the word of God and understood Ezra's explanation of its meaning for them.

Reverence and joy—this is the appropriate response whenever the scriptures are read and interpreted in the assembly of God's people. Particularly those of us who are actively engaged in the proclamation and interpretation of God's word should be aware of its immense value for the people of God. For in order to share this treasure with others, we must first receive it ourselves. Like Jacob, who wrestled with the Lord by the ford of the river Jabbok and would not let go until he received a blessing, so the preacher wrestles with the scriptures until a blessing is given—a life-giving word to speak. The regular experiencing of such blessings is one of the greatest joys of the preaching life.

As one can only come to name the riches any treasure chest contains by taking the time to examine it carefully with the proper tools and experience, so it is with the scriptures. Preachers must take the necessary time to dwell with the word if they are to identify the riches they hold for God's people. Through this dwelling with the word we preachers put ourselves in a place of blessing. To understand the kind of dwelling with the word that is most fruitful for one who is preparing to preach it, it is helpful to consider the time-honored practice of dwelling with the word known as *lectio divina,* or sacred reading. This method of wrestling with the scriptures until one receives the blessing of a life-giving word has been a regular part of monastic life since the dawning of the Middle Ages. Over the years, this practice has entered the main-stream of Christian life, being taken up by many who believe that through the Church's inspired writings God provides a lamp for our feet and a light for our path.

Basically, the practice of *lectio divina* works like this. One begins by reading the text, preferably out loud. The text is read slowly until a word or phrase grabs the attention of the reader. At this point the person stops reading and begins to reflect on that particular word or phrase, continuing for as long as the reflection is fruit-ful. The result of the meditation is the receiving of a word, a gift of understanding that is of real significance in guiding one's journey to the kingdom of God. Quite naturally, the receiving of this word creates a desire in the person to embrace it and to live by it. This desire, then, moves one to offer a simple prayer that God will help bring it to fulfillment. At times, God may respond by drawing the person into a wordless sharing in his divine life, through the grace of contemplation. Then, according to the time one has available, one takes up the reading of the text again following the same proce-dure. This fourfold process of reading, meditation, prayer and contemplation pays rich dividends for those who practice it. Through it one receives the blessing of a life-giving word.

I think it is helpful to look at the process of working with the scriptures in preparation for preaching as being similar to the practice of lectio divina. The major difference is that the goal of lectio divina is personal while the goal of working with a text for preaching is communal. In other words, when we approach a text for preaching, it is always as part of the community for whom we will be preaching. As preachers, we seek a life-giving word not just for ourselves, but for our entire faith community.

## Reading the Word

In liturgical settings where the scriptures are read before preaching, it only makes sense to begin our preparation with a careful reading of those biblical texts that will precede our preaching. Such a liturgical structure implies that the preaching will flow from the scriptures. In describing the relationship between the readings and the preaching in a liturgical setting, the "Constitution on the Sacred Liturgy" of the Second Vatican Council states, "By means of the homily the mysteries of the faith and the guiding principles of the Christian life are expounded from the sacred text . . ." (No. 52) Obviously, this can only happen if one begins with the reading of the biblical texts!

As we ready ourselves to read these texts, in addition to saying a prayer for God's assistance, it is important to remember who will be hearing the scriptures. It is helpful to spend a little time visualizing them, seeing them in our imagination, not only in the pews but also in the context of their lives. Such an exercise really helps us bring our congregation with us to the text as we take up its reading.

Since the texts will be read out loud in the assembly, it makes sense that we read them out loud, if possible. It also makes sense, at this point, to read from the particular translation that will be used in the celebration of the liturgy. As we read the text over, perhaps certain words or phrases will jump out at us as being of special significance for the people of our faith community. As in the personal practice of *lectio divina,* when this happens we will stop reading and begin to meditate on that particular word or phrase.

## Meditating on the Text

When meditating on a word as preachers, more is involved than a simple mulling over of things in our own minds. As a representative of the community, we bring the rich resources of the community with us as we "chew" on the meaning of a particular word or phrase, over and over again, like a cow chewing its cud. In the process, maybe we will recall the special significance attributed to this word or idea by some of the great preachers and theologians of past generations. It's possible that we will have a recollection of the special impact that this particular phrase or concept had on some important figure from the Church's history. Of course, we will also reflect on the reason that this particular word has captured our attention now.

As we reflect on the biblical text in this way, it is helpful to jot down these particular remembrances and insights along with any questions that arise as to the meaning of a word or phrase. Since this reflection is communal in nature, while we may be moved to offer a little prayer as we receive certain insights, we also realize that this prayer will only be completed in the community's response to the reading and preaching. As in the individual practice of *lectio divina*, when we complete our reflection and prayer at this particular stopping point, we take up the reading of the text until another word or phrase demands our attention.

However, unlike the individual practice of *lectio divina*, when we have completed this reflective movement through the texts, we are not yet finished. Following our initial engagement with the texts we will consult the writings of those who have devoted their time to the study of these texts, such as commentaries, bible dictionaries, word studies, and alternate translations. Since the preparation time of preachers is limited, perhaps it is best to begin this "extended reflection" by consulting one good commentary on each text. Then if we deem it necessary to explore a particular word or concept more fully we can turn to other available resources.

Since we will be preaching for a particular community it is also helpful to receive direct input from members of that community. This is the surest way to know how the texts speak to others in our faith community. For this reason, some preachers include as a regular part of their preparation process a study of the readings with a group from their faith community. Often the questions, observations, and personal experiences shared in such study sessions really help to clarify the connections between the texts and the congregation.

## Receiving a Gift and Sharing a Gift

If this extended reflection on the text is done with the kind of openness and thoroughness I have just described, it will undoubtedly require a few hours over the course of a couple days. Yet it pays rich dividends for us. Like the man in the Gospel who, upon finding a pearl of great price, was willing to sell all he had to buy it, preachers will discover that the time and effort they put into their engagement with the scriptures is a small price to pay for what they receive.

Depending on our own personal circumstances, the particular texts being considered, and the resources available, one aspect of our dwelling with the word often will be more profitable than some of the others. At times during our meditation on the text, sparks will be flying and light bulbs popping as insights come in powerful rushes. On other occasions, such meditation will fail to yield even a brief flash of light. But, then, as we consult a commentary, suddenly the clouds of "cluelessness" will part, and we will be greatly enlightened by the work of another. There will be still other times when our conversation with members of the assembly removes the "log in our eyes" so that we are able to see some implication of the text that we have never seen before. Since we never know which part of the process will yield the most fruit, it is important that we remain disciplined enough to go through the entire process each time we prepare to preach.

Usually this process of dwelling with the word will result in many rich insights into the God of life and the life of faith. Some of these will be of personal benefit to the preacher, while others will relate to the faith community. While it may be tempting to share all of them because they are all so good, it is important to avoid this temptation. This is true, first of all, because most of our preaching has some time limitation, for reasons of liturgical balance and for the sake of charity.

Also, not every insight the preacher has is appropriately shared with the congregation. After all, everyone doesn't need to know that the preacher has decided to remove the candy dish from her office because her own particular temple isn't reflecting the gracefulness of the Spirit as well as it once did!

And most importantly, not every insight we receive from our dwelling with the word should be shared because sharing too many may well keep the people from receiving any! In the book *Contemporary Christian Communication, Its Theory and Practice*, James F. Engel reports the results of a study done among churches in the Chicago area. People were polled as they left, being asked the simple question, "What was the main point of the sermon?" Over half could not remember the main point of what they had heard or even articulate a significant point. One factor always evident in such cases was that there was no main point. The preaching had no clear focus. In other words, because these preachers spoke of many things, the people left with nothing. Conversely, when the preaching focused on a single, well-developed theme, the people usually were able to remember it. Though it may be hard to contain our enthusiasm and choose a single theme, genuine love for our people demands it. And we will undoubtedly have plenty of opportunities to preach on the other themes on other occasions.

All this suggests that after we have finished our interpretive work with the biblical texts, there is still some work to be done. Now we must take the insights we have jotted down throughout the process of our engagement with the texts and prayerfully discern what the particular focus of our preaching will be. A few questions will help in this discernment. First, is there a specific word that has emerged from the scriptures that seems especially important for our faith community at this particular time? Second, is there a unifying theme that runs throughout the scriptures that the liturgy clearly intends to be our focus? Third, is there a particular theme that we are strongly moved to preach? The more "yes" answers that are given for a particular theme, the more strongly we should consider it as the focus for our preaching. All things being equal, i.e., if the needs of the community and the integrity of the liturgical cycle are being served, we should usually go with the theme that excites us the most, since this will definitely give a boost to our preparation and our presentation.

The point is that at the end of our dwelling with the word we must have a clear focus, a unifying theme, that can be expressed in a single, simple sentence. This will enable us to pass on something of great value from what we have received through our dwelling with the word. It is a great joy for us to receive such gifts from God. And it is an even greater joy to know that, by God's grace, we have something precious to share with those we love.

## A Preacher's Experience

Though I believe that one of the keys to consistently good preaching is to allow the preparation process to unfold over several days, I have never been able to bring myself to begin reading the texts for next week's preaching on Sunday. Though I love to preach I also find preaching to be hard and exhausting work. So after preaching a couple of times on Sunday morning, I need to turn off the homily producing part of me and let the batteries recharge.

But I'm back at it on Monday. Sometime during the day I set aside time to read and reflect upon next Sunday's lectionary texts. I always begin with the Gospel, since it is usually the most accessible. Also, when it comes to thematic connections with the other lectionary texts, the Gospel usually serves as the natural vortex for those connections. However, before I begin reading, I take a moment to pray, asking for the help of the Holy Spirit in my discerning of the word that the Lord would have me preach. As I pray, I allow images of the people of my parish community to come to mind, seeking to be aware of the important things that are going on in their lives. I conclude this brief period of prayer by commending the whole process of preparation to the Lord, that it may truly serve his loving purposes.

When I pick up the lectionary, I realize that I am bringing much more to the text than just a blank page. In addition to my congregation, I am bringing with me things that I have learned about the biblical texts, perhaps their historical contexts, various interpretations that have been given to the text, the existence of textual difficulties, or the significance the text has played in the Church's theological tradition. I am bringing with me great saints and notorious sinners who were either inspired by the text or stumbled over it. And I am bringing with me my own history of engagement with the texts as a dweller with the word and as a preacher. If we are going to be truly open to a fresh hearing of the word through these texts, it is important that we are mindful of whatever baggage we bring with us as we approach them.

So with whatever I bring with me I take up the reading of the text. I read it out loud at a fairly natural pace. Let's say it is the Gospel from the twenty-eighth Sunday in Ordinary Time, Year B—Mark 10:17-27. As soon as I begin to read it, I realize that I have read this text many times before. I have read commentaries on it. And I have preached on it.

When I get to Jesus' words, "Why do you call me good? No one is good but God alone," I am stopped dead in my tracks. I know I have wrestled with these words before. And I discover that I still have some unresolved questions. "How could Jesus say this? He was good. He was God incarnate. Yet the man didn't know this. So did Jesus say this for his benefit? Or wasn't Jesus' own understanding of his identity developed enough to know that he truly was God incarnate?" I wrestle with Jesus' words, going round and round, and finally, realizing that I am getting nowhere, I decide to get some help from commentaries later.

But for now, I get back to the reading. And in the very next sentence I am halted again. I wonder: "Why is Jesus answering a question about how one inherits eternal life by speaking of the commandments? Any good Christian knows that we are not saved by works of the law. Doesn't Jesus know this?" Remembering a little about what comes later in the text, I conclude that this is a set-up. Jesus is leading the questioner on to a deeper understanding. So I continue on with the text.

I pause briefly over the words given in reply, "Teacher, all of these I have observed from my youth." And I think to myself, "Was this man really being honest with Jesus? If so, he was certainly a better man than I am." I also think of the people in my congregation and conclude that he was a better man than just about all of us. Maybe in my homily I should address the issue of working a bit harder at keeping the commandments ourselves!

I no sooner get back to the reading than I am delightfully stunned as I hear myself say, "Jesus, looking at him, loved him." I have always been deeply moved by these words. Somehow they seem to surprise me every time I read this Gospel. I wonder why the text speaks of Jesus' love for this young man at this point. Is it because Jesus knows the struggles this young man is in for and so his heart goes out to him? Or is it simply because Jesus has a natural liking for him? Is his love for this young man different from the love Jesus has for me and all others? I don't know the answer to these questions. But as I prepare to move on with the text, I realize that, at the very least, Mark wants us to know that Jesus' response to the young man will be made out of love. And I realize that this is true of what Jesus says to each one of us. I wonder if perhaps my homily should convey this message.

I smile as I read the words "Go sell what you have, and give to the poor and you will have treasure in heaven; then come follow me." Of course, I knew they were coming. But these words have some special meaning for me. I cannot read them without remembering one of my favorite saints—Antony of the Desert. For it was in the hearing of these words as a young man that Antony had experienced a personal call. Through this Gospel God spoke to Antony's heart in a way that led him to sell his possessions, give them to the poor, and devote himself completely to following the Lord. I think of his solitary life in the desert, devoted to prayer and fasting in utmost simplicity. I remember how this life transformed him into a man of great charity and sanctity, who had a powerful impact on those who came in contact with him.

I ask myself how I have responded to this Gospel text in my own life. I feel uncomfortable about having so many possessions and occupying myself so much with things of no real significance. What would Antony think of me? What would he think of so many of the people in my congregation who are caught up in the accumulation of material possessions? How would they respond if I were to tell them to give up their pre-occupation with possessions and to become more fully occupied with God? Then some people in the parish come to mind who do live simply, give much to the poor, and are intensely devoted to following Christ. I try to imagine what Jesus would say to the people of my parish about all this. Should this theme of doing what is necessary to follow Jesus be my focus for preaching? At least I would have the example of St. Antony to share with them.

Coming back to the text, I read of the young man's response to Jesus' words. I can see him in me, in my family, and in the people of my faith community. We all have heard the words of Jesus calling us to simplicity, generosity and radical obedience. I understand the young man's sadness and sense that part of my own sadness and the sadness of so many of my people is very much like his. Should I speak to this in my homily?

As I take up the reading again I do not have to pause over Jesus' saying about how hard it is for the wealthy to enter the kingdom of God since my reflections have already made that clear to me. But I do stop to consider the response of the disciples who were "amazed" at his words. I remember a little of what I have learned about the ancient Hebrew view of possessions. Riches were considered by many as a sign that one was favored by God. So it is easy to see why the disciples would be struck by Jesus' words, which seemed to suggest that riches may actually keep one from being in God's favor. And I realize that many in my parish community will experience a similar kind of consternation over Jesus' words. Is this something I need to help them understand in my preaching?

As I read the words that follow I find myself remembering a visit from a member of my congregation many years ago. He was the owner of a successful business, and quite wealthy. In the midst of a pleasant conversation he asked, "What do you think about the passage in the Gospel where it says that it is easier for a camel to pass through the eye of a needle than for a rich man to enter the kingdom of God?" I can't remember my answer, but I will never forget the question. It was asked with utmost seriousness. And it is a question that could certainly be asked by many people in my present parish community. Should I speak to this in my preaching? What would I say?

I remember something from past reading suggesting that some believe that "the eye of a needle" was the name of a well-known gate in the wall of Jerusalem that was too small for heavily laden camels to pass through. But I realize that most of my congregation will think of a sewing needle unless I tell them differently. However, as I continue on with the reading it seems to me that it really doesn't make much difference. The disciples certainly experienced it as a very radical saying since they asked one another, "Then who can be saved?"

I move on to the final words of the reading. Initially as I speak them I get a warm feeling within. I recognize them as words I have spoken before. "For human beings it is impossible, but not for God. All things are possible with God." Yet as I ponder the meaning of these words in this context I realize that while I believe them I am not quite sure how to apply them. I become aware of my own uneasiness with the wealthy and my own tendency to judge them harshly. Yet I do know many wealthy people who are generous and who follow the Lord with more faithfulness than I can often muster. Perhaps I should focus on the relationship of wealth to the kingdom of God in my preaching. It is certainly an important issue in our society today.

As I conclude my reflective reading of the Gospel I suspect that because I have been so fully engaged by this text, it will provide the thematic focus for my homily. However, I suspend this judgment as I proceed with a similar reading of the other texts. I recognize the obvious connection between the Gospel and the reading from the Book of Wisdom, which portrays wisdom as being of much greater value than worldly riches. As I read the text from the Letter to the Hebrews I do not immediately recognize a connection to the Gospel. But I do think it portrays the word of God in a most glorious way. I ponder the meaning of the word of God being living and effective. I am mystified by what it means to say that the word of God is able to "discern reflections and thoughts of the heart." Usually I think of the word of God as something we use in our discernment of things. I don't usually think of it as doing the discerning itself. I realize that there is something of great importance here. But I also know that I need some help from the commentaries to come to a sense of genuine understanding.

The next day, I pull from my shelves whatever commentaries I will use this time around. As usual, I work with a commentary on each reading that I haven't used before and supplement it with notes from others that I have collected over the years. I enjoy working with the commentaries and find some material that is helpful. Most of what I read confirms my initial reflections on the text. As I guessed, Jesus' assertion, "No one is good but God alone," has received plenty of attention from interpreters from the earliest days. Out of the various viewpoints expressed, the one that seems most commonly and persuasively held is that Jesus was simply drawing attention to the fact that God is the absolute good we all must seek. Of course, the clear implication that the wealthy young man will find that absolute good by following Jesus shows the special connection between Jesus and God. One issue has been clarified.

By far the most significant part of my study of the commentaries centers on Jesus' answer to the young man's quest for eternal life, "Go sell what you have, and give to the poor and you will have treasure in heaven; then come follow me." Most of the commentaries cautioned that Jesus was not making some general statement to the effect that everyone has to give up their possessions to follow him but that we must all set aside whatever it is that keeps us from following him. I find this clarification to be very helpful. I also find myself being drawn to preach on this particular part of the Gospel.

My access to commentaries on the reading from Wisdom is not nearly as extensive. Somewhat to my surprise, I discover that this text does not go nearly as far as the Gospel in calling its readers to a radical choice. Commentators frequently make the point that the author of Wisdom wants the reader to know that while one should pursue wisdom for its own sake, the obtaining of external goods will inevitably follow the obtaining of wisdom. So it is not only a way to God but a way to earthly riches as well. I make a note of this as it may be of some use in preparing the homily.

I move on to commentaries on Hebrews. I discover that the text does indeed ascribe a very active role to the word of God. The word reveals what is true about the listeners as well as what is true about God. As I consider this I see a connection with the Gospel. The words of Jesus to the rich young man certainly revealed what was true about them both. I note this and then close up shop for the day.

That evening at our weekly study of the Sunday readings I gather with fifteen parishioners to discuss the readings I have been working on. Beforehand I have reviewed the notes from my own dwelling with the word and my jottings regarding possible themes. As sometimes happens, I come to the study with what by now is a pretty well defined thematic focus for my preaching: Jesus calls us to set aside those things that keep us from following him completely. Many times I come to this gathering without any sense of the focus or direction of next Sunday's preaching. But this week, I'm really feeling drawn to preach on this particular theme.

We begin with the Gospel. I ask: "What's going on in the Gospel? What do you think of the rich young man? How do you understand Jesus' response? How do you relate to it in your own life?" As expected, the discussion focuses on the rampant materialism in our society. Several participants speak of how they see possessions turning people away from God. A few brave souls even share some of their own struggles with this. Then I ask the group, "What do you think Jesus would say to you if you asked him what you had to do to gain eternal life?"There is silence. I ask a clarifying question, "Do you think that the thing that keeps you from really following Jesus is your love of possessions, or is there something else that steals your attention away from him?" After a briefer silence one says, "Going to all my kids' ball games." A few nod in agreement. Another says, "My need to do well at work usually consumes me so that I have little left for Jesus." A third person says, "My anger towards some people often keeps me from following Jesus." And so the conversation goes.

We consider the other readings. In our discussion of the reading from Wisdom someone notes the connection between the Gospel's call to radical obedience in following Jesus and the pursuit of wisdom as the most important thing. In our sharing on the Hebrews reading, someone makes the same connection with the

Gospel that I had recognized earlier. The word helps us to discern what keeps us from following Jesus more fully and faithfully. She even points out that we have experienced this very thing tonight during our study session. I lead the group in a closing prayer.

As we part company, I am sure that I will focus on the theme I had tentatively formulated before the meeting began. I have received plenty of confirmation regarding its importance for our parish community. And I have a clearer sense as to how this Gospel connects concretely with the lives of our people. Of course, things don't always go this way in terms of establishing a thematic focus for preaching. Sometimes I come to the study group with one idea and by the time it's over it has become clear that the needs and interests of our people in connection with the texts demand a different focus altogether. At other times I come with no clear sense of thematic direction. And sometimes I leave with none.

This experience of dwelling with the word in preparation for preaching is both personally and homiletically enriching. God speaks to me in so many different ways throughout this process. It provides a constant stimulus to spiritual growth. It drives me to continue developing my knowledge of the scriptures. And it adds to the excitement of preparing to preach for the Sunday assembly. This weekly dwelling with the word is truly one of my greatest joys.

## Chapter 4

# THE JOY OF CREATING SOMETHING GOOD

THE joy of receiving a word to share is indeed a wondrous thing. Yet it brings with it a challenge that will not let preachers sit and bask in the glory of it for long. For the word imparted to them through the lengthy process of scripture reading, study, prayer, meditation and perhaps even group discussion must now be imparted to their worshiping assemblies through the relatively few minutes allotted for reading and preaching. This can be a rather staggering thought, to say the least.

Of course, the preacher knows that the word is God's to impart. Yet the preacher also knows that those through whom the word is imparted can do much to make a congregation either disposed or indisposed to receiving it. A joke or a story without any clear connection to the word may send the people into a world of far off thoughts and images from which they may never return. An example that offends the sensitivities of the worshipers will hamper their hearing more certainly than a pair of earplugs. A little too much technical language from the biblical and theological fields may quickly convince all but a few that today's message from the Beyond is beyond them. Too large a dose of the familiar may lead to the quick judgment that they've heard it all before. Anyone who has spent much time on the pew side of preaching knows that what preachers say and how they say it has a great deal to do with what people may or may not hear.

So along with the joy of receiving a word to share comes an awesome task. How can I share this word of life in a way that will help my people receive it? This is the fundamental question that lies behind all preaching. Having received the creative word of God, the preacher must now be creative. Summoning all skills natural and acquired, the preacher must now fashion something that will help others receive this life-giving word.

## The Craft of Preaching

Of course, we must never underestimate God's ability to work in strange and mysterious ways. If the Lord can make an ass speak so that a human can understand it (Num 22:22-30), then surely the Lord can communicate his word through preachers who have made their pulpit ramblings about as difficult to decipher as the sounds normally emitted by Balaam's beast. However, God's obvious preference over the years has been to work in less quirky ways. It is truly a testimony to

God's love for us that God works most often through the work of his people. God honors us by calling us to use our abilities in ways that will assist in the accomplishing of his work.

So it is with preaching. Before it is God's work, it is just work. The preacher is engaged in the plying of a craft. It is the craft of opening minds and hearts. As with any other craftsperson, the preacher must learn to use a wide variety of tools. And from the tools that have been mastered, the preacher must discern which ones will most effectively open the minds and hearts of a particular group of worshipers to receive a particular word. Will it be a story that leads to laughter? The reporting of statistics with the raising of an eyebrow? A poem recited in melodious tones? A stunning image moving into a whispered prayer?

What tools will most effectively open the minds and hearts of the people this time for the receiving of this word of life? This is a question that only a true craftsperson can ask. It requires the kind of skill and experience that is only acquired through observation, practice, and a genuine desire to create something beautiful and serviceable. That preachers come to recognize that they are engaged in such a craft is of utmost importance. There is no room for the kind of casualness or sloppiness in preaching that gives the impression that what is being done really isn't all that important. Nor can preachers afford to neglect the finer aspects of the craft requiring creativity and skillful presentation. After all, preachers do not work in a vacuum. They are involved in a battle for people's minds and hearts. All kinds of skilled craftspersons are working to persuade people to adopt truths contrary to the Gospel. Because of this, preachers must do everything possible to become excellent craftspersons themselves.

In his usual persuasive manner, Augustine made this very point in his great work on preaching titled, *On Christian Doctrine:*

"Since, then, the faculty of eloquence is available for both sides, and is of very great service in the enforcing of either wrong or right, why do not good men study to engage it on the side of truth, when bad men use it to obtain the triumph of wicked and worthless causes, and to further injustice and error?" (IV.3)

## The Basic Elements of the Craft

Many excellent books are available that treat the various elements of the preaching craft. Some of the best comprehensive texts I have used over the years are Craddock's *Preaching,* Burghardt's *Preaching: The Art and the Craft,* Buttrick's *Homiletic,* Long's *The Witness of Preaching,* Troeger's *Imagining a Sermon,* Wallace's *Imaginal Preaching: An Archetypal Perspective,* and Lowry's, *The Sermon.* For those just taking up the craft, a good place to start is with the fine little booklet published by the National Council of Catholic Bishops in

1982 titled *Fulfilled in Your Hearing*. Though the work of many of these experts has shaped my understanding and practice of preaching, what follows is my own particular distillation and description of the most essential aspects of crafting a homily.

## Starting with a Clear Focus

The last chapter actually dealt with the first movement in the crafting of a homily. The preacher dwells with the word in a way that includes the community for whom he or she will be preaching. The goal is to have a word to share with the people. This word is to provide the thematic focus for the homily. I will not rehash the process of discerning that word. But I do want to reiterate the importance of concluding the process by writing out the thematic focus for the preaching in a single, simple sentence. This sentence should have neither connecting conjunctions that expand the focus nor any punctuation marks that allow for the addition of complicating phrases. The whole rest of the process of crafting the homily depends on the disciplined drafting of this focus sentence. If it is not stated sharply enough there will be too much room to ramble throughout the rest of the process. And it will quite probably end with the wasting of the congregation's time, since they will leave without anything substantial enough to hang on to.

## Identifying the Purpose of the Homily

In addition to sharply articulating the thematic focus of the homily, it is also important to clearly identify the purpose for preaching this particular message. Do we want to strengthen the people in a conviction already held? Do we want to challenge them to go one step further in their walk with the Lord? Do we want to teach them something? Do we want to help them to see how they have strayed in some way from following Christ? Or do we simply want to help them to rejoice in the good things God has done for them? Knowing what we are trying to accomplish in the preaching of a particular message will help us determine how best to develop the structure and content of that preaching.

## Determining the Approach

The possibilities of how a homily can be structured are multitudinous. The thematic focus and purpose of the preaching will certainly give direction to the approach taken. The scriptures themselves may also provide some guidance in this regard. After all, if the message and purpose flows from the readings and the readings were structured to convey it, then someone already considered the matter of approach — under the guidance of the Holy Spirit! So, if we are wise, we will be open to receiving such guidance from the biblical texts.

However, our particular gifts for expression may be quite different from those used in the biblical texts.

Also, the people and the setting may be quite different from those considered by the biblical author when writing the text. So in addition to the scriptures, it is helpful to become acquainted with the particular approaches taken by those who are considered past masters of communication, with contemporary communication theory through books and workshops, and to observe the work of professional communicators on television, including commercials.

One good basic rule of thumb is that when trying to strengthen people's commitment to something they commonly hold to be true, a more direct or deductive approach is a good way to go. But when trying to move people to embrace something different from what is commonly believed or practiced, a more indirect or inductive approach works best. The deductive approach begins with the stating of a commonly held conviction and then moves on to present material that supports the conviction. We might call this the cheerleader approach. The cheerleader begins with the assertion; "Our team is number one." To this the people may initially respond with a nod of assent and a somewhat subdued "yes." But then the cheerleader adds, "We have the best players." To which the people respond with a bit more spirited "Yes!" The cheerleader continues, "We have the best coaches." At this, the fans stand and reply with an even more vigorous, "Yes!!" Then the cheerleader shouts, "And we have the best fans." This leads to roaring applause and a thunderous

"YES!!!" By the time the cheerleader reiterates the initial assertion, "Out team is number one," everybody is thrusting their arms into the air with index fingers extended and cheering at the top of their lungs. Now, while a preacher may not get quite this response from a Sunday assembly, this approach of stating what we believe followed by compelling reasons as to why we believe it can be quite effective when that belief is already commonly held.

But what if we are trying to help people embrace a truth that requires some significant change in their way of thinking and living? In this case, the deductive approach is not nearly so effective. Beginning our preaching by stating a conviction that people do not commonly hold produces immediate and often very strong resistance. It creates an air of suspicion that will make people disinclined to consider any argument presented in support of the preacher's conviction. In such situations a more inductive approach works much better. This approach begins with the presenting of common experiences or commonly held convictions that are intended to move the people toward the embracing of the word the preacher has been given to proclaim.

What is required here is not a cheerleader but a salesperson. The salesperson doesn't begin by stating a conclusion. Rather she might say something like: "Everyone drinks water." Of course, almost everyone can agree with this. Then she might go on to say, "The studies indicate that the impurities in city water systems may cause long term health problems." And the people perk up a little more, since they have all heard of such things. The salesperson adds, "Our children are so precious, we don't want to take any chances whatsoever with their health." And many a person's head nods in agreement. Finally, with the minds and hearts of the people thus prepared to consider something different from what they have ever done before, the salesperson is ready to present that viable alternative. "I have on sale today, for a very reasonable price, a filter that attaches to your faucet and is guaranteed to remove all the impurities from the water. This will safeguard the health of your precious children." No doubt there will be some takers. The inductive approach is the best way to go when we want to break through resistance and move people to change. And since much of preaching is a call to conversion, this approach will probably be used often.

However, at times our preaching will have other purposes. If we want to help our people see how a particular biblical teaching will help them overcome a common difficulty, we might take the approach set forth in Milton Crum's book *Manual on Preaching*. First, we describe the biblical situation and show how it is similar to our present situation. Then we identify the conflict arising in the biblical situation and show how it is similar to what we experience now. Finally, we present the biblical resolution to the conflict and show how the biblical answer can help us overcome this same difficulty today.

This by no means exhausts the possibilities of how we might structure a homily in light of our thematic focus and intended purpose. Books on preaching and careful observation of various kinds of effective communication that we experience from day to day are also helpful. But regardless of how much we read or observe, if we are going to be most effective in our preaching then we must take the time to do our own prayerful and creative work. We must discern, in the midst of all the possibilities, what approach will be most effective in light of the message, the purpose, the people, and our own gifts as preachers.

Though this can be very hard work at times, genuine joy often springs from such caring and creative effort. It is the joy that any craftsperson experiences when an idea of something that will serve people well begins to take shape. When the thematic focus, the purpose and the basic structural approach are brought together into a creative union that promises to bear much fruit, the preacher is often caught up in a rush of joy. But this joy usually lasts only a moment. For there is quite a bit more work to be done if this promising start is going to find fulfillment in the preaching of the homily.

## Letting the Creative Juices Flow

Since there is a good bit of creativity required in the craft of homily preparation, it is helpful to build into the process an exercise that will quicken our creative impulses. A good way to do this is to brainstorm, simply jotting down anything that comes to mind that seems related to the theme, purpose, and approach we have established. Perhaps we will remember a movie or television program, a joke received in an e-mail from a friend, a saying on a bumper sticker or a billboard, a painting, or a comic strip. Maybe we will recall some statistics from a magazine article or a song we heard on the radio.

If we allow ourselves sufficient time and can move into a relaxed setting, it is amazing what rich and varied resources can be gathered in this way. For many preachers this is a most enjoyable exercise. However, if it is also to be serviceable, the ideas must be recorded on paper or on tape since even the best of them can fall back into that vast sea of thoughts from which we pulled them if we don't secure their capture!

## Fleshing Out the Form

Once the fishing expedition is completed the time for recreation is over. We must now get back into a more disciplined mode of working. It is helpful at this point to set before us the thematic focus sentence, the statement of purpose, and a brief description of the structural flow of the homily as we have envisioned it. In developing the homily's movement and material it is important to keep them in mind and not stray from any one of them.

As we begin to sketch out the basic flow of the homily we note in a sentence or a phrase what will be the gist of the beginning, each following movement, and the ending of the homily. Once this basic framework has been established, we can look over our brainstorming list, add anything that has come to mind since, and begin to flesh out each movement. I would suggest the following guidelines as being helpful for this part of the process:

• Make sure the beginning is engaging. It may well determine whether or not we will have anyone listening to the rest of the preaching. Also, make sure that the beginning has something to do with the theme and purpose of the homily. If we are tempted to begin with a joke or story that has nothing to do with the rest of the homily, we must stifle it. The opening material is intended to serve the homily, not the preacher.

• While the beginning should be engaging, it should not be so emotion-laden or disturbing that it actually prevents people from moving on with the homily.

• When sketching out the other movements of the homily it is usually best to vary the kinds of material used. For instance, do not use more than three examples in a row or give one quote after another. Vary the material so that people will be engaged both affectively and intellectually.

• The homily also should be varied in terms of intensity. A homily with too much intensity throughout will wear people out, while a homily with too little intensity throughout will put them to sleep. An ebb and flow of intensity, which allows the congregation to rest at points and reserves the greatest intensity for the end of the homily is usually most effective.

• Avoid the temptation to use material just because it's good even though it doesn't quite fit the theme and purpose of the homily. Also screen out material that does not connect well with the life experience of the people. In either case, people will be lost along the way.

• Never use material from conversations you have had during pastoral work that may be viewed as breaking a confidence. And never use potentially embarrassing material that involves persons in the congregation, family, or friends without first receiving their permission.

• Keep quotes from sources other than the day's scriptures to a minimum. Most congregations aren't nearly as interested in what others have to say as they are in what the preacher has to say. Even excessive quoting of the scriptures can often squelch the interest of the assembly. The homily is not intended to be a second reading of the sacred texts but rather a movement from those texts into the lives of the people.

• The sharing of the preacher's personal experiences can be used to good effect, as long as they serve the purpose of the preaching rather than the preacher, are related to the lives of the hearers, and avoid scandal or sensationalism. If used well, the sharing of personal experiences can establish helpful connections between preachers and congregations that demonstrate an understanding of peoples' lives and create a greater openness to receiving the message.

• Do not use materials taken from another source without acknowledging that this is the case. While specific names or publication titles do not always have to be noted, the outright stealing of material is no more acceptable in the pulpit than it is anywhere else.

• When it comes to the ending of the homily, it is important to conclude in a way that brings to focus the message and purpose of the preaching. It is best to vary the approach to the ending of homilies from week to week in order to maintain the congregation's engagement at this crucial moment and thus to ensure some continuing impact.

## Writing the Homily

Though some experts in the field of homiletics would argue otherwise, I believe it is generally a good idea for preachers to write out their Sunday homilies, even if they aren't going to use the manuscript in the actual preaching of them. This is a discipline that reaps many benefits. Writing a manuscript gives the preacher more of an opportunity to work on the fine points of the craft of homily construction. When a homily is written the preacher has something to look at, ponder, and evaluate. It is definitely a helpful tool for quality control. Writing it also helps to plant in the preacher's mind well considered language, sharp images, and clearly stated ideas that will greatly enhance the actual preaching of the homily. Manuscripts also provide a tangible record that can be used for an occasional evaluation of one's preaching. It also makes it possible to easily grant the requests of those who found the homily meaningful enough to ask for a copy.

If the work of sketching out the basic form and content of the homily has been done well, the actual writing of it is usually an easy and enjoyable task. And both spiritually and practically, it helps prepare us for preaching. As we reflect on how to say things in a way that will open our people to receiving the word of God, we find that this word is planted more firmly within us. And the hope of making a difference in the lives of the people we love, which builds as we build the homily, quickens our spirits.

When it comes to the writing, it is helpful to have a few guiding principles in mind. One thing to remember is that even though we are writing the homily, our intention is to end up with something to be spoken rather than read. So we must write as we speak rather than as we write! In other words, the language used will be the language of our conversations rather than our dissertations. The best way to ensure that there will be no theological insights imparted in our homilies is to fill them with theological jargon that is part of the everyday speech of only a few. When theological terms are used in preaching that are not part of the common language of the people for whom we are preaching they must be explained if they are to be of any service at all. The same is true of the various images and analogies we use. If they are to convey meaning to the people, then they must be familiar to the people.

Also, since we are dealing with oral communication, it is important to help people move from one part of the homily to the next through the use of good transition statements. In other words, we must connect where we have been to where we are going. When people are reading something they have the time to make such transitions themselves. But when listening to someone preach, if they have to take the time to think about the connection between what is now being said and what was already said, they will surely be left stranded somewhere along the homiletical highway. So transitional or linking statements are immensely helpful. And they are quite easily constructed.

## Preparing to Preach

When the manuscript is completed, the preparation for preaching is not. The sad reality is that many a good homily is preached without much good effect because the preacher who wrote it did not prepare to preach it. Preaching is not done on paper. It is an oral and visual engagement. So in addition to quality construction, the craft of preaching demands quality presentation. This means that preachers must know something about the principles and practice of oral communication. Particularly at a time in history when the kinds of oral communication that engage people on a regular basis are so polished and sophisticated it is essential that preachers devote time to this aspect of homily preparation. In what follows I will offer a few basic things for preachers to consider as they work on the actual preaching of their homilies.

## Speech and Physical Expression

Obviously if we are to be heard, our speech must be clear. But if we are to be heard for much longer than a minute, our speech must also be varied. A great deal of meaning is communicated along with our words through pitch, inflection, volume, and rate of speech. Through the high or low pitches of the voice are communicated mood and intensity. And if these pitches are not varied, the people grow weary of the sameness. They can become agitated or anesthetized, depending on the end of the range at which the preacher's voice happens to stick.

Inflection, that is, the emphasizing of particular words, can often give more meaning to a word or phrase than an adjective or adverb. "Jesus *loves* me," means he really, really loves me. But "Jesus loves *me*," means he loves even me. Of course the volume with which we speak also communicates a great deal. A softening of the voice may communicate tenderness. A whisper may be a request for careful listening. Or a whisper followed by a pause may be an invitation for prayerful reflection. An increase in vocal volume may suggest that something is worth getting excited about. But a monotone presentation throughout suggests just the opposite. How we say things definitely affects how people hear them.

So does the rate at which we say them. Much meaning and emotion is communicated, simply through the particular speed of our speech. The slowing down of speech suggests that something very important is being said and that people should listen carefully to every word. The speeding up of speech may mean that what is being said is of lesser importance. But if the rate of speech increases along with an increase in volume or the heightening of pitch it means that the hearers need to sit up and take notice!

As preachers communicate much through their voice, so they communicate much through their bodies. The simple movement of one's body toward or away from someone communicates engagement or distancing. So does the movement or non-movement of the hands. How one stands is often loaded with meaning. Standing erect, with feet firmly planted suggests formality while standing in a relaxed manner with a slight lean toward the people indicates informality. Endless fidgeting or unusual stiffness shouts of a preacher's insecurity and nervousness. This in turn makes the people nervous, so that all are worn out by the time the preaching has ended. Obviously, what we do with our bodies while preaching matters.

A great deal of meaning is also communicated by what we do with our faces. The lifting of an eyebrow may make a stronger statement than actually saying, "Oh, really?" A smirk may wordlessly add the strong opinion, "You've got to be kidding!" A scowl, however unintentional, communicates displeasure. On the other hand, a smile speaks a wordless, "I'm happy to be with you." Looking someone in the eye may say to that person, "I'm speaking directly to you," while failure to make any eye contact says, "I'm not very comfortable sharing this with you."

This does not mean that every movement of our bodies should be premeditated and well practiced. However, an awareness of what we are doing with our bodies while preaching is extremely important if we are serious about wanting to communicate most effectively. In this regard it helps to have someone videotape us from time to time and to get direct feedback from people who have been present for our preaching. This may be a bit humbling at times, but it is really the only way we can get a sense of what others are seeing and experiencing when we preach.

## Manuscript, Notes, or Nothing

One thing that preachers must decide before making any final preparations to preach has to do with whether or not they will use any written aids while preaching. Some will argue that all preachers ought to learn to preach without any written aids. From a communications standpoint it is obvious that if preachers are not looking at and handling written materials, they are freer to give their full attention to communicating with the people. And for those with the appropriate gifts and personalities this is certainly true. Preaching without any written materials gives a preacher much greater freedom of movement. Also, since there is no text, spontaneous adjustments in the preaching can be made more easily in response to feedback received from the people. However, preaching without any written helps does not work particularly well for those who are very introverted and often have to struggle for words. Nor is it effective for those whose thought processes do not move in a swift and orderly fashion. It is especially disastrous for those who are undisciplined or insensitive with regards to the amount of time consumed by their pulpit wanderings. In many cases having something written to help maintain focus and direction will increase the preacher's effectiveness.

But is an entire manuscript necessary, or will notes suffice? For many people, notes that include the main ideas for each movement of the homily, along with key phrases and important transitional sentences will provide all the help that is needed. While not permitting quite as much freedom as preaching without any written materials, using only notes does leave the preacher more room for spontaneity and adjustment. Of course, since notes must be placed somewhere, movements of the body will necessarily be more restricted. What is lost here, however, is more than made up for in the preaching of a homily that people will be able to follow and enjoy.

But what about preaching from a manuscript? Are there any preachers for whom this should be the preferred method? Definitely! Actually, there are many preachers who could benefit from using a manuscript. Again, the very introverted who often struggle for words, even to the point of blanking out on occasion will benefit from the use of a manuscript. Not only will they have the words at their disposal, but also they will be much less anxious about preaching. In itself, this will benefit the communication process, since people will not be distracted by the discomfort of the preacher. Also, many preachers who are gifted in the creative use of language feel more comfortable using a manuscript because they are ensured of saying things just as they intended. Certainly, those who are preaching in contexts where the precision of language and expression is of crucial importance are wise to use a manuscript. Finally, those preachers whose thought processes are impaired either temporarily or permanently due to various physical or emotional ailments will benefit greatly from the use of a manuscript.

## The Place of Preaching

Another important consideration in preparing to preach is where we will position ourselves in the liturgical space. Basically there are three options: from the ambo (pulpit), from the presider's chair, or freestanding in the main body of the church. Of course, each has its particular advantages. The ambo is the place designated in the worship space for proclaiming the Word of God. By preaching from the ambo a clear connection is made between the readings and the preaching. Also, most ambos provide a comfortable resting-place for notes or a manuscript. Preaching from the ambo suggests an element of formality and authority. And standing behind a structure that one can touch or even hold on to does provide the preacher with more of a sense of security than the other places. The most significant drawback to preaching from the ambo is that the structure itself partially separates the preacher from the people. It also limits the use of the body, thus diminishing somewhat the possibilities for enriching the communication through movement and gesture.

The presider's chair was a favored place for preaching in the early church. The chair was, for early Christians, the place where the scripture was interpreted by the one who presided over the community's worship. It was the place of authority. Though the significance of the presider's chair has diminished greatly over the centuries in many churches, it is still most often given a place of prominence in the liturgical space. And it still conveys a sense of authority. Interestingly, because one would normally preach from this place without notes, it also promotes a sense of informality and closeness. In fact, of the various options, this is the place for preaching that most fully communicates the blending of authority and intimacy. However, a chair is not a common place for preaching or speaking in our contemporary culture. With the exception of the judicial system, the sense of the chair being the place for authoritative address has been all but lost. Actually, the ambo is a clearer symbol of teaching authority in our culture. And if a sense of informality and closeness is what the preacher is seeking to project, then a freestanding position in the main body of the church is much more effective. Obviously, from a communications standpoint such preaching opens up possibilities that the others do not. One's whole body can be used to convey meaning, since it is in full sight of at least some of the people. Because the preacher is in closer physical proximity to the people a much greater sense of engagement can be established with them. Also, from a symbolic standpoint, this way of preaching most fully represents the movement of the word from the scriptures into the lives of the people.

This approach to preaching can be very effective. However, it is not without its drawbacks and potential pitfalls. The informality that naturally goes along with this approach does diminish somewhat the sense of preaching being a form of authoritative address. The sense of physical closeness and the intensity of contact can also be distracting to some people. Such preaching, to be effective also precludes the use of notes or a manuscript. And perhaps the most significant drawback is that often people focus more on the preacher than on the message. In other words, some people will be able to tell you what the preacher did but not what the preacher said.

So how do preachers decide the best place for their preaching? Sometimes the size and shape of the liturgical space and the available equipment will make the decision for us. If the liturgical space is configured in a way that most people would not be able to see us standing in their midst, then the freestanding approach within the main body of the church is out. This is also true if there is no portable microphone available. However, if for some reason a microphone is not available and the liturgical space is such that the only way the preacher will be seen and heard by everyone is to move closer to the people, then freestanding preaching may be the only good alternative.

But all things being equal, how does one decide? Basically, it is a matter of what will work best for the particular preacher. In other words, it is a matter of gifts, personal disposition, and comfort. If a preacher is comfortable speaking more informally, enjoys having some freedom of movement while preaching, and prefers to leave the notes in the study in order to be more fully engaged with the people, then freestanding preaching is a good option. However, if a preacher feels more comfortable standing behind an ambo, enjoys the security of a more confined space, and prefers to use notes or a manuscript, then the ambo is a much better place from which to preach.

The issue of the best place for preaching, then, is not determined in the abstract. Nor is it determined by fad or fancy. One cannot decide to preach from a free-standing position simply because someone else does it to great effect. Nor does the magnificence of the pulpit preaching of one necessarily translate into the life of another. Rather, the best place for preaching is determined by the particular preacher in the particular context. "Being the person I am, how can I best communicate the word I have been given to share with this assembly?" This is the question that each preacher must ask.

## Prepare to Preach by Preaching

Having considered some of the most significant background issues, there is still the important matter of how one prepares for the actual preaching event once the homily has been written. Simply put, the best way to prepare to preach a homily is by preaching it. Reading the homily over silently once or twice doesn't prepare one for preaching any more than looking a score of music over once prepares one for a piano recital.

Of course, it is a good idea to read the homily over once before moving on to a more intense preparation for preaching. But even this reading should be out loud and with as much expression as possible. It is important to hear how the homily sounds. During this initial read-through, the manuscript should be edited, making sure that the language is the language of speaking rather than reading, that transitions and main ideas are clear, and that the thematic focus is maintained throughout the homily.

For those who will be preaching from a manuscript, following the initial read-through and editing, a "preaching copy" of the manuscript can be prepared. In this working copy, the print should be sufficiently large and well spaced that words can be distinguished easily at a glance. To avoid having to look down too far and thus removing one's face from the view of the people, perhaps only the top two-thirds of each page will be used. Also, those parts of the manuscript that are of crucial importance, as well as those parts of the manuscript that often cause the preacher to stumble, will be highlighted in some way. Once the "preaching copy" of the manuscript is prepared, the preacher then preaches the homily again and again as one would preach it in the church, complete with full use of voice and body. The homily is ready to be preached when the preacher is familiar enough with the text that he or she is able to look at the people throughout, with only an occasional quick glance at the manuscript.

If one is going to preach from notes, then, after preaching through the manuscript once or twice to get a good sense of the overall flow of the homily, the preacher prepares a page or two of notes in a way that will facilitate their use in the pulpit. Perhaps lead sentences or main ideas will be in all caps and will begin at the left margin. Supporting material may be indented and noted in single words or short phrases with sufficient space between them to be easily distinguished. Words or phrases that the preacher wants to be sure to say in a particular way can be highlighted in a manner that draws the eye quickly to them. Once the notes are written, the homily is preached again and again, just as it will be in church, using only the notes, until the preacher has mastered the content and feels free enough to make spontaneous adjustments.

The preparation of those preparing to preach freestanding homilies can be similar. For many it will be helpful to prepare notes from the manuscript to help etch the movement of the homily more firmly in their minds and to use as a quick reference while practicing. However, because freestanding preachers do not use notes while preaching, the notes must be discarded at some point and the preacher must preach the homily just as it will be preached in the midst of the assembly. When the intended movement of the homily, complete with key ideas and phrases, is mastered so that the preacher is free to move and adjust to congregational response spontaneously, the homily is ready to be preached. Since the preacher has no written point of reference to look at while preaching, the best way to be sure the content of the homily has been mastered is by audio or video-taping.

## The Joy of Preaching?

This sounds like a great deal of hard work. And it is. But is there joy? Yes! (And I'm not just saying this because I'm writing a book titled *The Joy of Preaching*.) It is not possible to practice any craft for very long if one finds no joy in the work that must be done to produce something of excellence. For this is where most of the time and effort is spent. So where is the joy in the midst of all this effort?

The joy is to be found in working language into something meaningful and beautiful. The joy is to be found in developing an approach to some aspect of God's word that promises to help people to receive it. The joy is to be found in learning to use our voices and bodies in ways that enhance the meaning of the words we have so carefully crafted. The joy is to be found in thinking of how people will benefit from what we are preparing. The joy is to be found in the anticipation of helping to bring joy into the lives of people we care about very much. If the preacher is open to it, each moment in the practicing of this craft can be an occasion for joy.

## A Preacher's Experience

It is now Wednesday morning. Having completed my work with the scriptures for the Twenty-eighth Sunday in Ordinary Time, Year B, I have arrived at the focusing theme for the homily: Jesus calls us to set aside those things that keep us from following him completely. I am excited about preparing this homily. Why? What purpose would there be in preaching such a homily in my parish community? I know there are many people in our parish community who have made serious compromises in their commitments to following Jesus than there are people who have made this their number one priority. It seems that the rich young man in the Gospel fits more into this category. He was a good person, believed in God, lived according to the commandments, but was not ready to give himself completely to God. Jesus challenged him to a conversion of life that would mean setting aside the thing that was keeping him from fully embracing God's call. I feel that this should also be my purpose in preaching for the people of my parish community.

Since my purpose is to challenge people to change, I know that a more indirect approach will work best. I will have to give them something that will connect with their own experience of hanging on to things in ways that keep them from receiving more important things. Then in some way I must show how following Jesus completely is the most important of all things. And I must end with an invitation that encourages people to do that very thing. I enjoy this kind of reflection. It is a combination of prayer and play for me.

With theme, purpose and approach in mind I now give myself over to the creative exercise of brainstorming. The play *Annie* that I saw recently flashes through my mind, particularly how Warbucks held on so tightly to controlling his financial empire and political influence that he hadn't been free to accept the thing he needed most—the love of a woman and a child. I think of the time I wasn't willing to set aside my pride and ask directions, so I ended up on the Staten Island Ferry rather than on the ferry to the Statue of Liberty. I think of the Hebrews whose clinging to their cravings for the creature comforts they once had in Egypt kept them from entering into the bounty of the Promised Land. I think of Jonah holding on so tightly to the words God had given him to speak that he wasn't able to experience the wonder of what God's mercy had worked through them. I think of the father of St. Francis of Assisi, who held on so doggedly to his possessions and parental authority that he lost his son. The thoughts flow freely, one after another.

Finally, I have a few pages of notes most of which I will probably not use in my homily. But it's been fun. And I'm sure there will be something here that can be used. I set the notes aside. For the rest of the day and night I simply let things percolate somewhere in my subconscious while I engage in many different kinds of activities both pastoral and domestic.

The next morning (Thursday) I wake up with the homily on my mind. An idea has emerged from some mysterious place. Perhaps it was triggered by remembering the conversation in our scripture study about materialism being so terrible in our culture. Initially some of us missed the point that other things might just as easily keep us from following Jesus. I imagine the Gospel scene once again only expanding it in my mind. I imagine a conversation in the crowd. People making remarks about the rich man and how he was tied too strongly to his riches to follow Jesus. I further imagine Jesus calling one of them over and conversing with him. The man, who is very poor, assures Jesus that he will give up all his money and possessions to follow him. But Jesus surprises him by saying, "That won't be necessary. What I want you to do instead is to go back into the village and tell the neighbor who accused you falsely of stealing his chickens that you forgive him. Then come, follow me." At first he is stunned. Then this man too goes away sad. He could give up his money, but he can't bring himself to set aside his hatred and forgive the neighbor who had wronged him.

It seems that I've got the opening to my homily. It is an interesting twist to the story, and in meaning quite faithful to the Gospel. From there I will be able to move to a reflection on that story. I will then move on to a discussion of some of the most common things that we cling to these days that keep us from following Jesus wholeheartedly. The last movement of the homily will speak of how we can find it possible to let go of those things to follow Jesus. I will recall how Jesus looked on the rich young man with love. I will conclude by proclaiming that Jesus looks on us with that same love and that, though difficult, we can let go of things because the Jesus who loves us will help us.

I am aware that I have not woven the other readings into the homily. I also realize that to do so I would have to force them in somehow. I would rather let them stand on their own as they are proclaimed in the assembly. The Gospel is rich enough in itself to be the source of hundreds of homilies. So I am content to proceed this way.

The overall plan of the homily has come easily this time. It doesn't always happen this way. Sometimes it is excruciatingly difficult to get the ideas to flow. The only consolation I have at these times is that often the homilies I labor over the most turn out the best.

The next day (Friday) I sit down at my computer and write the homily. (Good word processing programs make it so easy to add, delete, and move things around that I strongly recommend that preachers learn to use a computer for writing their homilies.) The homily goes pretty much as I sketched it out the day before. I print this first copy of the homily on the backs of used sheets of paper because I know that this is not the copy I will end up taking into the pulpit.

The next morning (Saturday) I read the homily over out loud. I clean up language to make it the language of speaking. I delete an example that may be too disturbing to some very vulnerable people. I add a few clarifying sentences. (And I thank God for my computer!) The homily is now ready to put into final form. Since I will be preaching from the ambo, I set up my pages so the printing starts near the top and ends about two-thirds of the way down the page. I double space and use a font large enough to read easily (for me Times New Roman, 14 works just fine). After printing it out I preach the homily from the text. Then I preach it again. I become more aware of the natural pacing and intensity of the material. I set the notes on my desk and stand in front of them, trying to be as expressive in voice and body movements as I will be when I preach for the people. This time I stop to underline words or phrases I want to emphasize. Then I preach through the homily again. This time I mark those sections that are difficult for me to move into or through, so my eyes can find them quickly on the page. After preaching through the homily several times, I have become familiar with the text so that I have most of it clearly in mind. I know where things are on the page so I can get whatever help I need from the text in a quick glance. After a prayer for God's help, I am ready to preach for God's people.

This is definitely hard work. But for me it is a labor of love. I love the work itself. I enjoy the creative reflection. I enjoy the writing and the editing. It is all part of the craft. Though the practice is not as much fun for me, I find inspiration in the hope that what I do will truly make a difference in someone's life. For me, this is all part of the joy of preaching.

## Chapter 5

# THE JOY OF SPEAKING
# OF WHAT WE LOVE

AT a recent school meeting things were particularly sluggish. The discussion was focused on fundraising. People were about as eager to speak as a man standing before a firing squad who has just been asked if he has any last words. Nobody was talking for fear they would get stuck doing something they didn't want to do. Eventually the fundraising issue was tabled and the chairperson moved on to the next agenda item which had to do with preparations for the football game coming up that Friday night. Suddenly the room came to life. It was as if the tomb had been opened and Lazarus had come forth! Parents began talking enthusiastically about the big game. It appeared that at any moment the mothers in attendance might break out into a cheer as they spoke of their football playing sons, their daughters on the cheerleading squad, their children in the band, and even those children who were just excited about going to the game as fans. It took a while for the meeting to be brought back to order for people had actually begun to enjoy themselves!

Of course they were enjoying themselves! We all take delight in speaking of what we love. Think of our everyday conversations. Those who love sports always seem to work the conversation around in that direction. Those who love to eat usually find a way to mention their favorite restaurants. Those who love reading will turn someone's comment into an opportunity to speak of a book they've read. And those who are in love don't require any opening whatsoever to introduce their beloved into the dialogue. When I think of my own daily doings I realize that I am always finding ways to work my wife and children into conversations. Let's face it, one of the greatest joys in life is to speak of what we love.

Herein lies the joy of preaching. It is an open opportunity for preachers to speak of what they love. We don't even have to be creative about working it into the flow of a conversation. It is something we are invited to do, expected to do, or even required to do. When we stand to preach, the people gathered around us actually want us to speak of what we love! They want to hear us speak of God, of God's people, and of the Christian life. We don't have to say, "By the way, I just happen to have a few pictures here." The people are waiting for us to paint a picture of the Christian life for them. They have come to hear us speak of God! It is our job to speak of what we love. What could be more wonderful?

## The Love of God

> Let him kiss me with the kisses of his mouth!
>  For your love is better than wine,
>      your anointing oils are fragrant,
>  your name is perfume poured out . . .

(Song of Songs 1:2-3a)

These are obviously words of love. In fact, the whole of the Song of Songs is a collection of such words. It is a book of love poetry as steamy and earthy as any that has ever been written. As such, it is an immensely valuable part of sacred scripture. It confirms that such feelings and relationships are a gift of God to be treasured and can be used to achieve God's good purposes for his people. At the same time, it is interesting how often the lovers of God have used the language of everyday life in the world, such as that found in the Song of Songs, to speak of God.

Though modern exegetes sometimes cringe at the thought, St. Bernard of Clairvaux wrote eighty-six sermon commentaries on the Song of Songs and not one of them had to do with the passionate, heart-thumping kind of love shared between a man and a woman. Instead, as preachers had for centuries, he found these earthy love poems speaking to him of his love for God. And who can blame a male celibate for hearing the words, "Let him kiss me with the kisses of his mouth" in a way different from that originally intended by the author? Surely God himself, in inspiring such writing knew that in new contexts the words would be given new meanings. St. Bernard himself says something like this in his very first sermon on the Song of Songs: "We must conclude that it was a special divine impulse that inspired these songs of his [i.e., Solomon's] that now celebrate the praises of Christ and his Church, the gift of holy love, the sacrament of endless union with God." (IV.8)

Throughout the centuries Christians have been unable to resist the impulse to find in words describing human relationships some connection with their experience of God. So St. Bernard sees in the words, "Let him kiss me with the kisses of his mouth" an expression of his desire to enter into a deeply loving relationship with God. It is the same impulse that led the group of nun's in the movie *Sister Act* to transform the words of the popular song "My Guy" into a song about "My God."

This is one of the great joys of preaching, to take the words of everyday life and use them to speak of God. When it comes to interpreting scripture, it is a good idea for preachers to let people know when they are ascribing a meaning to words that is somewhat different from the author's original intention. Even better, we can explain the connection between our interpretation and the original intention.

Fortunately, as preachers, our creativity doesn't have to go into creating opportunities to speak. Such opportunities are handed to us on a silver platter. So our creativity can be channeled entirely into using all the words and experiences at our disposal to speak of the God we love. This is what transforms the whole process of preparation, along with the preaching itself, into something joyous.

## The Love of God's People

"Then [Jesus] took a little child and put it among them; and taking it in his arms, he said to them, 'Whoever welcomes one such child in my name welcomes me, and whoever welcomes me welcomes not me but the one who sent me' " (Mark 9:36-37).

We cannot truly love God without also loving God's people. This is the point of Jesus' words and actions in the verses quoted above. In Jesus' time and culture, children were on the bottom rung of the social ladder. They were considered to be of little worth. By taking a child into his arms and equating the receiving of that child with the receiving of God, Jesus was declaring that every person is precious to God and should be treated as such. That God loves people so much is part of the reason we love God so much. And it is by loving God that we grow in love for others. Preachers who truly love the God of whom they speak will also love the people for whom they speak.

That as preachers we are given the opportunity to speak of the God we love for the people we love on a regular basis is a great privilege. And it is an even greater privilege to do so in some of the most significant moments in people's lives.

## HOLY DAYS

During the course of each year we are looked upon to preach on holy holidays. These are days when families will be gathering to celebrate because God has done something extraordinary, something of immense significance for their lives. Yet often so much is put into the celebrations themselves that the significance of what God has done is all but lost. The fact that our churches are often filled to overflowing on such days gives us exciting opportunities to connect the people we love with the God we love by reminding them of what God has to do with their celebrations. These are truly privileged moments.

## BAPTISMS

Another such privileged moment for preaching is when the sacrament of baptism is being celebrated. Often this takes place in the context of a regular Sunday liturgy. This is an ideal setting for relating the gift God gives in baptism to the lives of those assembled. The trick here is trying to find a way to relate this most fundamental of all Christian sacraments to a particular Sunday's readings along with whatever special seasonal emphasis there may be. However, since baptism is the most fundamental of all the sacraments, the one from which the whole life of the Church springs, it usually doesn't require changing one's approach to preparing the Sunday homily. One can still begin with the thematic focus that emerges from the readings, though the fact that baptism is to be celebrated will certainly have something to do with the discernment of it. And some movement in the homily should clearly connect baptism to the focusing theme.

In those faith communities where baptisms are often celebrated outside the regular Sunday liturgy, preaching can be a bit more challenging. It may seem strange to say this since, on these occasions, the liturgy is focused specifically on baptism. However, several factors make preaching at such times a rather formidable undertaking. Often the number of people is relatively small compared to the Sunday assembly. And it is not unusual to have a much higher percentage of those gathered be people who are not regular churchgoers. Add to this the likelihood of energetic children being present who are not familiar with what constitutes appropriate behavior during liturgical celebrations. Quickly, what at first seemed to be an ideal setting for preaching is turned into a preacher's nightmare. Often the minister of baptism is tempted to simply pour and punt, leaving the preaching for a more opportune setting. And yet, for the love of God's people, even in the midst of something akin to the primordial chaos, preachers will find a way to speak of the God they love. After all, what more appropriate setting is there to speak of the One whose Spirit hovered over the waters at the dawn of creation, preparing to bring forth life?

So what can be done to make preaching effective? For one thing, the homily must be very brief. People who are not used to being present for preaching, particularly children, will not be able to endure longwinded homilies. Also, because of the smallness of the assembly and the intimacy of the sacrament to be celebrated, the preaching will have to be a bit more informal than usual. This is especially true if there are a number of children present. If they are going to be attentive, then they will have to be engaged on a very direct and personal level. This also means that the preaching will be more concrete and conversational.

As with any other preaching, the particular focus of the baptismal homily will depend on the reading(s) selected and the particular people for whom the homily is being preached. Basically, the preacher is given an opportunity here to help those present to understand more fully the great gift God gives his people through the sacrament of baptism and the community's responsibility for nurturing this gift in those to whom it is imparted. Because there are several important symbols used in the celebration of baptism, it is often helpful for the preacher to incorporate an explanation of those symbols into the homily. In this way a brief bit of preaching is extended through the remainder of the celebration in the consciousness of the people as the various symbols are employed. Also, pointing out the various symbols to be used is a good way to engage the interest of the children present.

If we fit our preaching appropriately into the context of this celebration, it can truly benefit the people present. For some it may become an invitation to share life with God more fully. For others it may become a moment of recommitment. For others it may simply be a joyous affirmation of their faith in the God of life. So whether within or outside a Sunday liturgy, the celebration of baptism does present us with a wonderful opportunity for preaching.

### MARRIAGE

A similar opportunity presents itself during the celebration of marriage. This is a celebration that has immense significance for the people of God. Of two people becoming one in marriage St. Paul says, "This is a great mystery, and I am applying it to Christ and the church" (Eph 5:32). In other words, Christian marriage is a reflection of the unifying love that forms Christ and his people into a single body. Yet this celebration, so laden with spiritual significance, is often set in a context that makes preaching difficult.

This is another ritual event where a large percentage of those present may not be churchgoers. Many may not be familiar with the church's ritual or with what is appropriate behavior in sacred space. Often there are a number of people in the assembly who have little interest in the religious dimensions of the celebration.

In addition, there are frequently a number of distractions that do not exist in the usual Sunday worshiping assembly. The wedding party is often dressed in unusually fine clothing. The groom and the bride, especially, are clothed in ways that grab people's attention. Candles, flowers, ribbons and bows have been added to the space to dress it up in ways that are intended to catch the eye. Sometimes, little children in wedding costume wander down the aisle during the processions and then around the church for the rest of the ritual, creating one diversion after another. Photographers, videographers, and wedding coordinators are all busy doing their jobs, adding even more opportunities for distraction. Brides and grooms are frequently fidgety with nervousness. Parents are weeping. A great party is awaiting everyone immediately following the ceremony. Needless to say, this is another setting in which many preachers are tempted to simply bless and recess. However, to do so is to miss a wonderful opportunity for preaching.

Since there is so much that is distracting at weddings, and since there are often many people present who are uncomfortable in the unfamiliar confines of a church, it seems that this may well be a setting where preachers cannot assume that they begin with the people's attention. Seldom do people come to weddings looking forward to the homily! So this may well be a preaching situation where it is necessary to begin with something that is attention grabbing and quickly connects the preacher with the people. Does this mean that the preacher should begin with some joke about marriage that has nothing to do with the real message of the homily? No! Does it mean that the preacher should begin with cute little stories about the bride and groom that have absolutely nothing to do with the thematic focus of the preaching? Double no!!

So what does it mean? It means that like any other preaching event, the beginning of the homily actually ought to be part of the homily. Interesting stories from the lives of the bride and groom are wonderful ways to begin wedding homilies because they do draw the attention of those present. However, the preacher cannot sell out here. Demonstrating how cute and endearing the homilist can be is not one of the criteria for determining the content of any homily, even one preached at a wedding. In the Roman Catholic Rite for Celebrating Marriage During Mass, the rubrics state that, drawing the homily from the scriptures, the preacher "speaks about the mystery of Christian marriage, the dignity of wedded love, the grace of the sacrament and the responsibilities of married people, keeping in mind the circumstances of this particular marriage" (22).

Clearly this rubric acknowledges that there is a personal dimension involved in this kind of preaching. Everyone has come because two particular people are getting married. So the preaching must acknowledge this in some clear way. At the same time, as with all other preaching, a wedding homily flows from the scriptures. For this reason it makes sense for the couple to be involved in the choosing of the readings. Obviously, the occasion already provides a focus for preaching, since the readings have been chosen because of what they say about marriage as it relates to God, to the lives of God's people, and, especially, to the life of this particular couple. So, having grabbed the people's attention with an engaging opening, the preacher builds on it, speaking of the gift, grace and responsibility of the married life in light of the scriptures that have been proclaimed.

If it is done well, a homily in this context can ignite some peoples' interest in the Christian faith, lead others to a recommitment to the married life, and support those who have honored the gift of Christian marriage their whole life long. Though the bride and groom may themselves be too nervous to listen during the liturgy, it is likely that someone will relate to them something of what the preacher said at their wedding, if the preaching is done well. Also, the preacher can give the couple a copy of the homily to read together when they are a bit less nervous. Because of their festive nature and immense importance for human life, weddings can be delightful and very fruitful occasions for preaching.

## FUNERALS

The other common context for preaching that connects profoundly to a particular event in the life of Christians is the funeral liturgy. This is truly a privileged place for preaching. No experience in life affects people more than the death of a loved one. At the time of a funeral those closest to the one who has died are still moving about in something like a surreal fog. They are functioning but disoriented, present but in a way that is strangely disconnected from what is going on around them. This is the way the body and mind usually respond to this particular wound of love. Even those who are not as closely related to the deceased are profoundly affected. They too are wounded by the obvious pain of people they care about or by their own forced glimpse at the crushing reality of death.

Preachers who love their people cannot help but be profoundly affected themselves. As they come before the people to speak of the God they love, they bring their own wounds inflicted by current and past experiences with death. But they also bring with them the healing words of life. Of all the settings for preaching outside the Sunday liturgy, this is the one that cries out the most for the sharing of a word that will help God's people continue on their journey toward the kingdom. Though the joy of preaching is experienced differently in this setting, it is very real.

Of course, preaching at funeral liturgies does present unique challenges, as well as unique opportunities. Here is another liturgical setting where many people attending will not be regular churchgoers. Yet, unlike weddings, where the religious dimension of the celebration has a tendency to be swallowed up by other things, the focus of the funeral is clearly spiritual. Death has a way of bringing people face to face with ultimate concerns. So those coming to funerals expect to hear words of faith. They have come looking for some assurance that there is something beyond the dark coldness of death.

But they also have come because a particular person has died. Many come to bear witness to the importance of that person's life for them. Unlike a wedding, however, where the life of the couple is automatically lifted up before the people by their visible presence and participation in the liturgy, the funeral can only do this for the deceased through symbol and speech. The homily can be seen, in part, as a special occasion for lifting up the life of the deceased before the people. Thus, in a funeral homily, spirituality and personality are tied together more closely than in any other of the Church's celebrations.

The challenge of preaching in this setting is to work with this dynamic of the spiritual and personal in a way that shortchanges neither. It is essential to realize that the people's emotions and attention are focused on the person who has died, because, as in any other situation, we can only bring them to God by engaging them where they are. In other words, if we do not speak enough of the deceased, many people will not be able to really hear us when we speak of God. Besides, the gift of human life is precious. Each person is such a wondrous expression of God's creativity and love that we cannot really speak well of God in this context without also speaking of the one in whose memory the community gathers.

Does this mean that what is called for in this setting is a eulogy? Absolutely not! A eulogy is a speech that focuses entirely upon a particular person and his or her special contributions to life. And this is never the purpose of preaching. In whatever context it is taken up, preaching is for the proclaiming of God's word. Thus, the *General Introduction to the Roman Catholic Order of Christian Funerals* states, "A brief homily based on the readings is always given after the gospel . . . but there is never to be a eulogy. Attentive to the grief of those present, the homilist should dwell on God's compassionate love and on the paschal mystery of the Lord, as proclaimed in the Scripture readings. The homilist should also help the members of the assembly to understand that the mystery of God's love and the mystery of Jesus' victorious death and resurrection were present in the life and death of the deceased, and that these mysteries are active in their own lives as well" (27).

Of course, it should be obvious that one can only show how "the mystery of God's love and the mystery of Jesus' victorious death and resurrection were present in the life of the deceased" by speaking of that life. There is no such thing as a generic life or a generic death. So there can be no such thing as a generic funeral homily. People are present at funerals because of a particular life and death. In fact, many are so focused on it that the only way they will be opened to the mystery of Jesus' victorious death and resurrection is if it is clearly connected to the mystery of the life and death of the one whose funeral is being celebrated.

As each individual is unique, so the connection between the word of God spoken through scripture and the divine word spoken through each life will reflect that uniqueness. So each funeral homily will involve getting to know about a person's life and death. Then, in each case, the movement of relating a person's life to the scriptures and to the lives of those in the assembly can be done with freshness and creativity.

Obviously, along with creativity, the preparation of funeral homilies requires sensitivity. First, it requires sensitivity to those who will be present. We do not want to give those who mourn any suggestion that their faith is inadequate by ignoring their profound sense of loss and speaking only of our faith in the resurrection. On the other hand, we don't want to focus so much on the sadness of the situation that we make it impossible for people to experience the joy and consolation of faith. The preacher can only know the appropriate emphasis to give on each by becoming aware of the circumstances surrounding a person's death and the effect this has had on people.

Second, preparing funeral homilies will require sensitivity to the truth. It is scandalous to portray a notorious sinner as a saint. And it is even more scandalous to tell things that cast the deceased in a negative light in order to be amusing. As with any other preaching situation, there are temptations here that must be avoided for the love of God's people. Compassionately honest may be a good way to describe the best approach to funeral homilies.

Third, preparing funeral homilies will require sensitivity toward those present who are not active church members. It is always uncharitable to take advantage of the good intentions of people to accomplish our own purposes, however good those purposes may be. Funerals are not the time to preach heavily loaded evangelistic homilies that threaten those present with the fires of hell if they don't turn their lives over to the Lord before they die. This is no way to treat guests in the Lord's house. It is true that funerals provide a wonderful opportunity for evangelization. The prospect of death definitely has a way of opening people to conversion. However, the most effective evangelizing in this context is done through well-prepared homilies that acknowledge in fitting ways the life of the one whom people came to commend to a loving and faithful God.

When a preacher has a sense that the funeral homily has helped people to view the death of a loved one in the context of the dying and rising of Jesus, thus enabling them to move from devastation to celebration, this becomes an occasion of deep joy. In fact, the preaching of funeral homilies can be among the most fulfilling experiences in one's entire ministry.

## The Love of the Christian Life

> "The kingdom of heaven is like treasure hidden in a
>     field, which someone found and hid;
> then in his joy he goes and sells all that he has and
>     buys that field."                    (Matthew 13:44)

Most preachers have a passion for the Christian life. Even those of us who don't live it particularly well,view the life of following Jesus as the greatest treasure of all. We are aware of its challenges. And we know of its promises. We believe that nothing is of greater importance. The life of following Jesus is a glorious life. How blessed we are to be able to speak of it, to be expected to speak of it, even to be required to speak of it. Our work is to speak of something we love. If this is not joy, what is?

What does it mean to be a Christian, to follow Jesus in the various contexts of life common to the people we serve and of which we are a part? We search the scriptures. We pray. We reflect. We sit in silence. We wait for a word that will come as a light for our path. And when the word comes, we try to find a way to speak it so that our people will be illumined by it too. There is a secret joy in this, one that is known by the preacher alone. It is the joy experienced by Jacob, when after wrestling with God at the river Jabbok, he went on his way limping but blessed. The receiving of God's word and relating it to life is hard work. It often requires a great deal of wrestling. But it is blessed work because the message does come.

To speak of this treasure in a way that helps others find it never diminishes what we have received, but only increases it. It is such a great joy to see others grow in their love for the Christian life through our speaking of it. And this joy is increased even more when we realize that through our preaching we have gained some traveling companions. We have gained brothers and sisters with a common purpose and passion. This is something experienced by almost every preacher who has preached for very long. As we speak of the life we love, others confirm our own choice to follow Christ. It is indeed a life worthy of our greatest love. And our hearts are filled with joy.

## A Preacher's Experience

On Monday mornings the prospect of coming up with another homily for the upcoming Sunday often leaves me feeling weary and burdened. I trust in the Lord's promise of rest for all such people that come to him. But I also know from experience that rest will not come for me until I have done a good bit more laboring. So breathing the heavy sigh of those who must be creative on schedule, I pick up the scriptures and begin to read next Sunday's texts. And quite often, before my time for reading is exhausted, I receive some initial bit of homiletic stimulation. Often it's no more than that little boost one receives from a strong cup of coffee taken in midafternoon when the eyes begin to droop. At other times, it is like the rush of excitement that comes when the doorbell rings and some eagerly awaited package has arrived. Something about God, or the life we are called to live as God's people, grabs hold of me. I am challenged, consoled, chastened, or cajoled as God speaks to me through the sacred texts. And I know that this word will do the same to others if I can only proclaim it in a way that will open them to receiving it.

As I think of this I find myself being flooded with new energy. What was initially a burden is suddenly transformed into another opportunity to speak of the God I love to the people I love in ways that may help them to live the life I love. Of all the things I do as a priest, there is nothing that is a more constant source of renewal, hope and joy than the time I spend preparing and preaching homilies.

Of course, there is an increased element of burden and excitement when I prepare to preach on those great holy days like Easter and Christmas. I know that the church will be filled like the overstuffed stomachs most of us will have later in the day as we gather in our homes around holiday tables. And I do feel a great responsibility to give this great crowd something to eat, something that will enrich their celebration of the feast, and perhaps even the rest of their lives. It doesn't bother me that many will be present who are seldom seen in church. In fact it delights me to think that I will have a chance to speak to them of the God I love and of the wondrous life he calls us to share with him. I am an eternal optimist. After many years of preaching I still prepare my homilies with the hope that they will become an occasion for significant or even profound conversion in the lives of at least some who will be present.

Other privileged moments are a bit less dramatic but come with greater frequency. Often I celebrate baptisms outside of Mass where small groups of families and friends gather around the font. As parents try to keep their babies from crying and as someone in the background with a video camera strains to get it all on tape, I read a little Gospel about Jesus' own baptism or about his invitation to let the children come to him. Then very briefly I try to speak of the wondrous thing that is happening this day as we prepare to celebrate God's adoption of our little ones as his sons and daughters. I speak directly to those present, usually only a few feet away. I tell them plainly that their presence is a pledge of their willingness to help these little ones learn what it means to be children God. And they know I mean it. Perhaps I have suggested how terrible it would be for these little ones to be adopted by such a wonderful Father but never come to know about it because those who presented them for this adoption didn't make it known to them. Though my preaching at baptisms often only takes a few minutes, it is the only regular chance I get to preach so informally and directly to people in an intimate setting. The crying babies don't bother me. Nor do their fidgeting siblings and cousins. This is part of the privileged moment, speaking of God and the life to which God calls us in a context that has a bit more recognizable reality to it than the usual Sunday assembly does. For me it is a real joy.

Weddings are a different story. This setting is not as comfortable for me, especially when the wedding becomes too much of a production. When the threshold of modesty and moderation are transgressed, my threshold for how much I can give of myself to such a celebration is pushed to the limit. Also, when many people are present that seem to have little respect for religious ritual and show thoughtless disregard for what is appropriate behavior in a holy place, I am greatly distracted and feel the energy draining out of me. Fortunately, this is not the case with all weddings.

But regardless of how I happen to be feeling about things, I do recognize this as a privileged moment for preaching.

No matter what the motivation, people have come to a wedding in a church, and so church is what they will get. And I want to give them church at its best. In addition to a fine liturgy, I want to speak to them in compelling ways of the love of God that is reflected in the love of Christian husbands and wives. I want to speak to them of how this committed love gives life to a couple, to their families and friends, and to the world.

I know that a wedding assembly is often a tough crowd to reach, so I try to find something that connects to the readings that will grab their attention at the very outset. Usually it is something biographical from the life of the couple being married, or from my own marriage. And it works most of the time. Addressing the couple directly at certain points during the homily also helps to keep them focused. But as with all other liturgies, the preaching is for the entire assembly and I try to make the most of this privileged moment. It is truly a joy when, as I preach, I see on the faces of people or in their interactions with those around them, some sign that the word I have been given to proclaim is breaking through to them. Thankfully, this happens often.

Of all the settings in which I preach outside the Sunday liturgy, funerals are my favorite. This may be surprising to some, but probably not to most preachers. There is a personal element involved here, a bond of Christian community, of shared life and faith that is experienced with greater intensity in this setting than in any other. Often I am called upon to preach at the funerals of people I do not know. In these cases I have to arrange for some significant interactions with the family and friends of the deceased prior to the funeral. I feel that if I am going to preach well, then I have to know something about the deceased. I need to get a sense of the person's life, its essential characteristics, and its impact on others.

Even if I know the deceased well, I still meet with family and friends of the deceased in preparation for the funeral. Though it may begin slowly, usually after a few minutes of talking about their loved one the stories are flowing freely, families are interacting in ways that are bringing them closer together than they have been for a long time, and I am brought into this intimate circle of relationship. This is one of the greatest of all the privileges I am granted as a preacher. To be welcomed into these intimate interchanges where people express their grief and love for another human being is an awesome thing for me.

The other thing that makes preaching at funerals especially fulfilling is that people are usually expecting and even wanting to hear me preach. They want to hear of the dying and rising that is at the heart of our Christian faith and how their loved one has now come to participate in it more deeply. They want to hear words that honor a life that was a gift of God for them. They want to hear words that give them some assurance that there is cause for consolation and hope in the face of this particular death. They want to receive a word that will help them face the prospects of their own deaths.

I enjoy preparing homilies for funerals. I enjoy looking at the readings as they relate to the life of a particular human being. I find it a delightful challenge to look at the Gospel through the prism of a person's life and see how the word is reflected there. I find myself wanting to minister to these grieving people I have come to know and love. I want to do all I can in my preaching to help them get in touch with the significance of their loss, with the unique gift with which they have been blessed in the life of the deceased, and with the joy and celebration that accompanies the commending of a loved one to the God of life. When I sense that my preaching has truly helped them more fully embrace the God I love in such a difficult time in their lives—well, there is no greater joy for me.

## Chapter 6

# THE JOY OF THE CROSS

THE very first rite celebrated with those seeking initiation into the Roman Catholic Church is called the Rite of Acceptance into the Order of Catechumens. This rite marks the beginning of a journey, taken up in the midst of the faith community. It is a journey that leads to the font and the table, where through water, spirit, and eucharistic communion these persons will become part of the Body of Christ. After greeting the candidates and hearing their spoken desire to embark upon this sacred journey, those individuals who will travel along with them as their sponsors impart to them the sign of their new way of life. They make the sign of the cross on the candidates' foreheads, then on their ears, eyes, lips, hearts, shoulders, hands, and feet. Finally the presider makes the sign of the cross over the whole lot of them. In this way it is made clear to both candidates and congregation that the way of Christ is the way of the cross. Through this powerful rite, it is etched indelibly into the consciousness of catechumens that being incorporated into Christ means taking up the cross.

To the uninitiated, this may sound terribly morbid. But it is not. Mysterious, most certainly. Serious, to be sure. But there is nothing morbid about the taking up of the cross. Surely the catechumens knew this before they came seeking admission into our community of faith. After all, we meet in a place where the cross is clearly visible as a central symbol of what we are about. And they asked if they could join us! This could have happened only because somewhere along the line they heard the Christian proclamation that we are saved by the power of the cross.

Through the gracious mystery at work in the preaching of the Good News our catechumens have come to believe that taking up the cross of Christ is the way to eternal life. They are not so naïve as to think that the way of the cross is traveled without great struggle and pain. But they have come to see that these sufferings are a small price to pay for the splendor of the risen life. This is the hope-filled message that has brought them to seek admission into the community of cross bearers: by dying to ourselves and embracing the cross of Christ we will come to share in his resurrection. And so they receive the cross with smiles on their faces and tears rolling down their cheeks because they have come to recognize it as the way that will bring them to the greatest of joys.

This is the fundamental reality of the Christian life. There are no exceptions. It is never a question among Christians as to whether or not the cross will be taken up. Rather, the point of discernment for individual Christians is how the cross will be taken up in the unique context of their lives. As Christians are gifted differently so they must give of themselves according to those gifts. This is what defines their particular pathway to joy. And preaching is one of those pathways.

As Jesus' own preaching led to the cross, so will the preaching of all that follow him. There is no other way. To speak of the joy of preaching we must speak of the joy of the cross. This is not always easy for preachers to remember, especially when we are laboring under the weight of the preacher's cross, or being nailed to it. It requires much prayer and reflection to develop such mindfulness. Yet if we develop this awareness, we will discover that just as Jesus recognized his being lifted up on the cross as a moment of supreme joy, calling it his moment of glorification, so we can find a comparable joy in the sacrifice required of us. In fact, the more fully we give ourselves up to the sacrifices required by this ministry the more open we become to the exquisite joy to which the taking up of the cross leads.

## The Cross of Laboring under a Heavy Load

Letter carriers are not the only ones who are expected to make their deliveries on time, regardless of weather conditions, social crises or personal difficulties. So are preachers. However, unlike letter carriers, who only deliver what they have received from others, preachers must also generate what they deliver. The coming of

Sunday is not like the ebbing and flowing of human creativity. Sunday comes each week regardless of the preacher's proclivity for creativity. It comes in those weeks when ideas are so plentiful and profound that preachers must pare down the portions of homiletic gems they offer just to keep people from being overwhelmed by their pulpit potency. It also comes in those weeks when ideas are so scarce and sorry-sounding that preachers have to pan the streams of sermonic possibilities for hours just to come up with some little nugget of nourishment that will tide the people over until the ideas become bountiful once again. But the expectation that preachers will have something to say when Sunday comes is guaranteed. After all, preaching is our vocation. We know how important it is for our people to be nourished each week at the table of God's Word.

In addition to the hard work of coming up with something substantial to say each week and crafting it in a way that is interesting enough for people to be attentive, the act of preaching itself is quite labor intensive. To stand before people we love and speak of things that are of the utmost importance, that may in some way make a difference as to whether or not they will come to life in the kingdom, requires a tremendous expenditure of energy. It is no accident that many preachers are quite exhausted by the time Sunday afternoon rolls around. They have given everything they had for the sake of their people in their presiding and preaching during the morning liturgy. Now they have nothing left. It is hard for those who do not preach to understand how exhausting it can be to carry this cross. But for those of us who preach regularly, it is not surprising that we sometimes grow weary to the point of exhaustion from bearing the weight of it.

## The Cross of Humiliation

Anyone who preaches long enough (and for some of us that is not very long at all) will say something unbelievably stupid from the pulpit. A common story is told among preachers of the young pastor who was looking for a good way to begin a homily on the importance of love within the family. As it happened he attended a mid-week service where a preacher spoke on this particular theme. His opening was most engaging. He began, "The sweetest, most wonderful, loving woman I ever held in my arms was another man's wife." Then after a brief pause, in which the entire congregation sat in stunned silence, he continued, "She was my mother." At this, smiles of delight broke out on the people's faces.

Seeing how effective it was, the young pastor couldn't wait to use this same opening in his homily on Sunday. However, knowing it was a rather sensational way to begin a homily he was a bit nervous. He began, "The sweetest, most wonderful, loving woman I ever held in my arms was another man's wife." The words had their intended effect. Unfortunately, the stunned looks on the people's faces rattled the young preacher so much that he couldn't remember the next line. Panicking, he continued, "And for the life of me I can't remember who she was."

Yes, there are times when, much to our chagrin, we preachers catch ourselves saying things in the pulpit we wish we hadn't said. There are also times when we will notice people in the assembly turning to each other and laughing. We wonder what in the world we said that was so funny, especially since we were intending to be quite serious. Did the words come out wrong? Did we naively use some phrase that has a much earthier connotation in the minds of the people than what we intended? Or are people just laughing at us because what we are saying or the fact that we are the ones saying it seems so ridiculous? Taking up the cross of preaching does lead to some humiliating moments.

However, there are much greater humiliations attached to the preaching life than being laughed at when we aren't trying to be funny. For instance, there are times when we marshal up all our homiletical skills and preach what we believe to be a stirring homily. We are sure that it will have a profound effect on the people. But as people leave church it is obvious by their avoidance of the subject or by the particular comments they make that they didn't have a clue as to what we were talking about. And suddenly the image of pulpit master is transformed into pulpit disaster!

At other times, people definitely get the message but don't like it. Disfavor with our preaching is expressed in many ways. Icy stares or angry glares meet us in the pews. People choose other exits following worship. A few may lecture us as others waiting in line to greet us look on. Angry phone calls may follow. Perhaps even anonymous hateful messages will be left on our answering machines or will come in the mail. At some point anyone who faithfully preaches the Gospel will suffer the humiliation of being ridiculed. This is painful enough when it comes from those outside the Church. But it is far more painful when it comes from the members of our own congregations.

However, the greatest of all humiliations for preachers are not those inflicted from without. The most humbling thing for most of us who preach is the simple fact that it is we who are preaching! In his delightful book, *Telling the Truth: the Gospel as Tragedy, Comedy & Fairy Tale*, Frederick Buechner begins with a story about Henry Ward Beecher. Reverend Beecher had come to Yale to deliver the first of the Beecher Lectures on preaching, which had been established in memory of his father. Up until an hour before the lecture, he had been unable to develop so much as an outline. It was while shaving within that hour before speaking that everything came together. Beecher's biographer notes that he cut himself badly while shaving that day. According to Buechner, this was most appropriate, since Rev. Beecher had become the center of a public scandal because of his relationship with the wife of one of his parishioners. Buechner concludes that "Henry

Ward Beecher cut himself with his razor and wrote out notes for that first Beecher Lecture in blood because, whatever else he was or aspired to be or was famous for being, he was a man of flesh and blood." This is part of the cross that all preachers must bear. Buechner sums it up well: "We all labor and are heavy laden under the burden of being human or at least of being on the way, we hope, to being human."

This is the greatest humiliation for most preachers: proclaiming the word of God though we are not God. We speak the word of truth, though we know that we have not always been truthful. We speak the word that calls people to faith, though we know that we have not always been faithful. We speak the word of love, though we know that we have not always been loving. We know that we are not worthy to speak of such things because the word of God has so often been contradicted in our own lives. At times we are aware that the people know this about us. At other times, there are deep secrets that we carry with us into the pulpit that are known by us alone. Often we feel that, perhaps more than anyone else in the congregation, we are the ones who need to be converted by the word we preach. Of all the humiliations we experience as preachers, there is no greater cross to bear than this.

## The Cross of Disappointment

All people experience disappointments during the course of their lives. Preachers are no exception. In fact, the cross of disappointment is taken up quite frequently by those who preach. What preacher doesn't know what it's like to step into the pulpit with great excitement on Sunday morning? We are ready to preach a homily that took a great deal of hard work to prepare and that promises to be quite effective. Then a baby starts to cry, or a child breaks loose and runs down the aisle, or some elderly person in the congregation goes into a lengthy chorus of loud, hacking coughs that is repeated with great frequency throughout the homily. The distractions mount, the preacher feels like throwing his hands up in the air or like throwing up. There are plenty of little disappointments like this in the preaching life. And there are some that are not so little.

As a young preacher in the United Methodist Church, only a few years into my ministry, I did something that I have since come to view as an abuse of the privileged place of preaching. I used preaching as an opportunity to express my own personal frustrations. I was preaching a sermon on the ministry of all believers. In that sermon I said, quite boldly, that one of the reasons so many ordained ministers end up leaving full-time ministry in the Church is that Sunday after Sunday they preach a word that they believe to be a matter of life and death, but it doesn't really seem to matter much to anyone. Nothing changes. The lives of people continue on pretty much the same. I honestly admitted that I felt this way at times. This left some of the congregation rather shaken. They were afraid that I was getting ready to leave them. The result was that I got something off my chest and for at least a couple weeks, the people were much more responsive to my requests for volunteers.

Though I would not encourage using pulpit privilege in this way, this incident does highlight one of the most difficult things we have to bear in the preaching life. We may put our whole heart and soul into our work. But often there seems to be a rather meager response. We know people in our congregations who are in trouble. We know people who are enslaved to sin. We know people whose spirits are broken and need to be healed. We want very desperately to help them. We prepare homilies with them in mind. We preach our hearts out. Yet nothing seems to change very much. At times we feel like Jesus looking over Jerusalem and saying, "Jerusalem, Jerusalem, the city that kills the prophets and stones those who are sent to it! How often have I desired to gather your children together as a hen gathers her brood under her wings, and you were not willing! See, your house is left to you desolate" (Mt 23:37-38). One of the heaviest crosses that preachers bear is the cross of unfulfilled hopes and disappointments.

## The Cross of Loneliness

"The cheese stands alone," says the old children's song "The Farmer in the Dell." So, often, do preachers. The truth is that the path many preachers travel is a rather lonely one. The preaching life itself turns even the most normal of us into something of an oddity. The truth is that, compared to the number of people in our churches, those of us who regularly step up to the microphone to preach the word of God are relatively few.

During my seminary days I spent a summer as chaplain to three campgrounds at Smith Mountain Lake in Virginia. I lived in a little trailer without restroom facilities. So I had to use the public restroom. Often as I approached the building I would hear laughter or crude comments coming from inside. However, when I walked in and people recognized me, the laughter and foul language stopped. The preacher was now in the building, which meant that people were a bit uncomfortable and no longer felt free to speak normally. Sometimes I found myself wishing that someone would cuss or tell an off-color joke after I entered the place just so I could feel like a regular human being.

Of course, it is no surprise that as preachers we will be looked upon as being a bit freakish by those who do not believe in the Gospel. Paul rightly said that the Gospel appears like foolishness to many. So we can count on the fact that those of us who preach it will be thought of as fools. Most preachers accept this reality, though it is difficult at times. However, far more difficult is the sense many of us have that our preaching sets us apart from a large number of those who believe in the Gospel. No, they don't think us foolish — only different. It seems that many people feel they must maintain a certain distance from us if we are to function for them as God's spokespersons. They treat us as though we are imbued with some aura of holy mystery that makes us as unapproachable as the God who resides in the holy of holies. Thankfully, not all our fellow Christians relate to us in this way. But there are many times when, as we step into the pulpit on Sunday morning surrounded by those we call our brothers and sisters, a wave of loneliness sweeps over us that is staggering. This is one of the painful crosses that many a preacher has to bear.

## The Cross of Sacrifice

The New Testament makes it clear that the basic pattern of Jesus' life is reflected in the lives of those who follow him faithfully. In the Book of Acts, Luke makes this point quite explicitly. Both Peter and Paul suffer because of their preaching in the name of Jesus. They are imprisoned, brought before councils, and ridiculed. Following this pattern, which is easily recognizable as the pattern of Jesus' own life, the ultimate sacrifice of their lives is anticipated. And the tradition tells us that it was accomplished as both died martyrs' deaths in Rome. While not all preachers reflect the sacrifice of Christ in their lives with such stark resemblance, all preachers will reflect it in significant ways. To take up the preaching life is to take up the cross of sacrifice.

In this chapter I have described the kind of sacrifice that seems to be common to all preachers. Obviously some will experience different aspects of this sacrifice more intensely than others will. But we all will experience them to some degree. We all will suffer the cross of hard work, of humiliation, of disappointment, of loneliness. All of us will give up something of our lives for the sake of preaching the Gospel, as did the one whose Gospel we preach.

But why do we do it? It should be no surprise that St. Paul has something to say about this, since he sacrificed more than most for the sake of preaching the Gospel. In Second Corinthians he proclaims, "We are afflicted in every way, but not crushed; perplexed, but not driven to despair; persecuted, but not forsaken; struck down, but not destroyed; always carrying in the body the death of Jesus, so that the life of Jesus may also be made visible in our bodies. For while we live, we are always being given up to death for Jesus' sake, so that the life of Jesus may be made visible in our mortal flesh. So death is at work in us, but life in you" (4:8-12). In other words, we take up the sacrifices associated with the preaching life because it is in this way that we unite ourselves with Jesus and carry on his saving work. The taking up of the cross of preaching is a profound manifestation of our love for the Lord and for his people. And because of this, it is a source of great joy.

## The Cross of Joy

In the first chapter of the Book of Revelation, John tells how he was on the island of Patmos "because of the word of God and the testimony of Jesus" (1:2). In other words, John had been exiled to this island for preaching the Gospel. He was certainly familiar with the sacrifices that go along with this ministry. Yet he also relates that it was on this island of exile, while he was "in the Spirit on the Lord's day," that he received the vision that became the Book of Revelation. It seems that far from distancing John from the Lord, the difficulties he experienced for the sake of preaching actually drew him closer, close enough to receive this most intimate and mystical communication.

This is what happens when people deny themselves, take up their crosses and follow Jesus. A deep bond is formed between them. It is the bond of those who suffer for love. It is the bond of those who care more about the well-being of their brothers and sisters than they do about their own well-being. It is the bond of those who suffer together for a glorious cause. It is this bond that forms all the followers of Jesus into a single body, intimately and mystically united.

The cross of preaching, then, is ultimately a cross of joy because it brings us together with our Lord and his people in the deepest of unions. It is the kind of intensely joyous union that can only be understood by those who together have sacrificed for the sake of something worthy of such sacrifice. It is somewhat similar to the kind of unity experienced by the members of a football team who have become all battered, bruised, and bloodied as together they fight on toward victory. Or it is like the intense unity experienced by firefighters who, wheezing from smoke-filled lungs, scorched and spent, continue to risk themselves in a common effort to rescue people from a burning building. Such self-sacrificing, common efforts forge the strongest of bonds between people. The joy of the cross, taken up in preaching, is that it creates such a bond between us, our Lord, and those who make up his body. It is the joy that comes from being united with the greatest of all persons in the greatest of all works.

## A Preacher's Experience

The ministry of preaching is not easy for me. Unlike many preachers, who dread the difficult chore of preparing homilies on a regular basis, I actually enjoy this aspect of the preaching ministry. I am a hermit at heart. Sitting alone in silence, studying, reflecting, praying and creating are things that come naturally to me. I love this part of the preaching ministry. The biggest cross for me is not preparing to preach but actually preaching.

The cross of laboring under a heavy load starts taking its toll on me the moment I realize that I will once again be standing before a group of people in a public setting. It is what might be called anticipatory anxiety. And I always have it. Of course the weight of this load increases a bit when I think that these people are actually hoping that I will have something to say worth listening to. Fortunately, the preaching itself requires such intense concentration that I no longer feel the stress of the situation much during the homily. It is after the homily has been preached that often, quite drained, I plop down into the presider's chair breathing a silent sigh of relief. It is finished! And quite often, so am I. This is especially true if I am preaching a homily that challenges the congregation to embrace some aspect of the faith more fully and that I suspect may disturb or even anger them. Since I am an extreme introvert, preaching drains the energy right out of me. It is hard work. So after two Sunday morning Masses I'm usually ready to "come away to a deserted place and rest awhile."

In addition to the cross of exhaustion, I have also experienced the cross of humiliation on many occasions. I have received occasional phone calls or letters from people who were upset about things that I really didn't say or even suggest. Indelibly etched in my memory is the chewing out I received from one of my best friends, who actually did understand what I was saying in a sermon one day and didn't like it! In front of a large number of people, who were in line to exchange greetings with me as they left church, in a loud, angry voice, my friend made it quite clear that he was offended by what I had said. He completed his tirade by warning me that I had better never say anything like that from the pulpit again! That was definitely a humiliating experience. Though I didn't agree with him or the way he handled it, I have been much more careful about how I say things from the pulpit ever since. A little humiliation of that sort goes a long way.

However, the greatest cross of humiliation for me is having to preach a word that speaks of a life I am not yet fully living myself. Sometimes I get the sense that because I say something from the pulpit people assume that I am speaking of what I have already mastered. The truth is that I have just as many weaknesses, limitations, failings, and doubts as most of the people for whom I am preaching. In fact, every time I preach I realize that I am speaking to many who are holier than I. What many people don't know is that most of my homilies are addressed to me first, challenging me to ongoing conversion and growth.

And do I experience the cross of disappointment? Of course I do. I experience it every time I feel I have not spent adequate time preparing a homily. I experience it every time I feel I have not done a good job delivering a homily. I experience it intensely when I feel I have something really important to say to the people and something happens to distract them. Perhaps a bee comes in through the window, creating a panic in the pews; or someone's beeper goes off; or parents don't have enough sense to get their screaming children out of church so the people around them can actually pay attention to what I'm saying.

I am especially disappointed when I preach a homily that I hoped would have a profound impact on the people but which actually results in little visible or verbal response. I am the kind of eternal optimist that steps into the pulpit each week hoping to open people so fully to the God who will speak to their hearts that there will be people in the church shouting for joy, weeping large tears of repentance, dancing in the aisles, or responding with thunderous applause. Needless to say, I am frequently left carrying the cross of disappointment.

I am also quite familiar with the cross of loneliness. It's not that the people in my parish don't love me. They do. I have received countless expressions of their love. It seems that most of the people even like me. My preaching is simple, down to earth, filled with stories and images that suggest that I understand something about the lives they are living. I share enough of my own life in my homilies to give people a sense that I am personally familiar with the kinds of struggles they experience while trying to be good Christians.

But I am still the one who stands in the pulpit and preaches the word of God. I am the one who speaks for the Church. I am the one who speaks of sin and conversion. I am the one who reminds people of their responsibility to live as witnesses for Christ. I am the one who speaks of mysterious things like the Incarnation and the Trinity, the angelic and the demonic, the dying and rising of Christ and his people. So while in some ways I may be quite a regular guy, at the same time I am like few other regular guys my people know.

As a result, most people can't help feeling a bit uncomfortable around me. I am a sensitive person and I am often quite aware of their discomfort. I even understand it. To be honest, the fact that I am a preacher even makes me uncomfortable with myself a good bit of the time! Though I know that people appreciate my presence, look forward to it, and even enjoy it, there is still, quite often, a sense of separation that is related to my being a preacher.

The preaching life does require us to take up the cross of sacrifice. We must give up our lives in many ways. Especially difficult for me is the sacrificing of time with my wife and children. I try not to make my cross theirs. But sometimes there is nothing I can do about it. If there is a football game on Saturday afternoon and I am preaching on Saturday evening, usually I am unable to go. Quite often on Sundays, for a few hours after church, I don't feel like doing much of anything. I know this frequently disappoints those in the family who have spent a quiet Sunday morning and are now eager to do something fun. Usually, I end up participating like a zombie or falling asleep in the car on the way to wherever it is we may be going. My preference is to ask if everyone can just wait an hour while I shut down and let my batteries recharge. I hate doing this, but sometimes I have no choice. I know that my embracing of the cross of sacrifice forces the members of my family to embrace the cross of sacrifice too. For me, this is one of the greatest crosses of all. Thankfully, they are supportive of what I do and usually accept the crosses they must bear on account of me quite graciously.

But is there any sense in which the cross of preaching is a cross of joy for me? Most definitely! I find myself often echoing the sentiments expressed by Jeremiah. "If I say I will not mention him or speak in his name any more, there is, as it were, a burning fire caught up in my bones, and I grow weary from holding it in and I cannot." Though I may moan and groan about the cross of preaching every now and then, the truth is that nothing gives me more joy than preparing and preaching homilies. When I surrender myself fully to this difficult work, I find that I am not only somehow in touch with my truest self but also in deepest communion with the Christ who is the great Preacher behind all preaching. Christ is the Word through whom all things were made. He is the Word that is proclaimed when the Gospel is preached. In my preparation and preaching of homilies, a union is forged between us that fills me with deepest joy. It is a joy that floods my life with meaning and purpose. It is a joy that transforms the difficult aspects of the cross of preaching into a fragrant bouquet that is offered gratefully to the God of life. For me the cross of preaching is most of all a cross of joy.

**Chapter 7**

# THE JOY OF
# THE COMING KINGDOM

WE used to have a sandbox in our backyard that was a frequent gathering place for the neighborhood children. Usually there were only a few playing there at a time. And things were generally pretty calm, just one friend playing with another. But on occasion a larger group of bigger people would invade the yard. Inevitably this horde of alien invaders would attempt to take over the sandbox, crushing whatever masterpieces our little children had created, and making a general mess of things. These neighborhood nasties enjoyed terrorizing little children. They wanted to leave no doubt in our children's minds as to who ruled the neighborhood. They strutted and taunted and threatened. But just when they thought they had established their reign of terror and could do anything they wanted to menace our little ones without consequence, a single word would be shouted—"Mom!" Suddenly a look of terror would come upon the faces of the terrorizers. They would jump out of the sandbox and run from the yard as fast as their legs could carry them.

That single word had broken their hold on the situation and put them to flight.

This is an image that preachers would do well to remember. For it embodies in a wonderfully simple way our belief in the power and promise of preaching. The Church's utter confidence in the power of the proclaimed word was expressed in a most remarkable way by Martin Luther in the sixteenth century. In his well-known hymn, "A Mighty Fortress is Our God," Luther writes:

> And though this world, with devils filled, should threaten to undo us,
> We will not fear, for God hath willed His truth to triumph through us:
> The Prince of Darkness grim, we tremble not for him;
> His rage we can endure, for lo, his doom is sure, One little word shall fell him.

Perhaps the most joyful aspect of the preaching life is to know that the word we preach is the instrument God uses to break the power of evil. It is the ultimate weapon that assures the victory of light over darkness, of life over death. Those of us who have taken up the cross of preaching have not done so because we enjoy looking foolish to those who are ruled by the "Prince of this World." We have taken up this cross because we know it is the very thing that puts the devil to flight. We take up the cross of preaching because it leads to the release of captives and to the resurrection of the dead.

Preaching is for us a joyous way of sharing in the paschal mystery. Sacrificing ourselves in union with Christ, we come to share even now in the full and eternal life he came to establish. Taking up the cross of preaching, we enter into that saving mystery. The Word through which the world was created is also the Word through which it will be redeemed. The word we take up in preaching is the very word that ensures the ultimate fulfillment of our constant prayer: "Thy kingdom come, thy will be done, on earth as it is in heaven."

In the nineteenth chapter of the Book of Revelation Jesus is described as being clad in a robe dipped in blood. And the name by which he is named is "The Word of God." The text goes on to say, "From his mouth comes a sharp sword with which to strike down the nations" (19:15). It is this sword that will be used to vanquish the powers of evil and to establish God's reign upon the earth. Though this ultimate victory is often portrayed as being the result of a bloody battle, what the author is speaking of here is the power of God's word. It is the preaching of the word that will ultimately overcome the resistance of the nations and the powers of evil. This is the sharp two-edged sword that proceeds from the very mouth of Christ. And this is what we take up in preaching. What can possibly be more glorious?

## A Preacher's Experience

It is true that no one has ever said as the result of my preaching, "I saw Satan fall like lightning from heaven." But during the course of my life I have witnessed the in-breaking of the Kingdom through the ministry of preaching. It is not possible for me to count the times that the sharp two-edged sword spoken of in the Book of Revelation has pierced my heart during someone's preaching. I have been shaken out of lethargy, lifted out of depression, empowered to break free from temptation, and inspired to give myself more fully in the Lord's service. I have been convicted of sin and have received the remedy for it. I have been filled with joy and sometimes have even felt a little of the love and peace that is the eternal atmosphere of the Kingdom. I have no doubt that the word of God is what will ultimately establish the coming Kingdom in all its fullness because it has already begun to open that Kingdom to me through the preaching of the word.

And thankfully, I have also seen the same thing happening in others because of the preaching I have done. On a fairly regular basis people thank me for some homily I preached because God spoke to them quite personally through it. Often people will ask for copies of a particular homily that moved them deeply, so they can share it with another in hopes it will move them too. Occasionally there have been some rather dramatic responses to a message I have preached. Perhaps a person has returned to active participation in the life of the Church after a long absence, or an addict has found the courage to seek counseling after having denied the problem for years, or someone who has held on to anger for a decade has finally been moved to forgive.

Yet most often, the glimpses of the coming Kingdom that result from my preaching are much less dramatic—the nod of a head, a sigh, the taking of another's hand, a smile, a brief silence shared by all, a smattering of laughter, a tear. Such things happen on a regular basis as I preach. And though nobody would say it this way, I experience it something like Satan falling like lightning from heaven. That "one little word" has felled him. In such moments, I catch a glimpse of the Kingdom that is sure to come. I enter the gracious mystery. This is the joy of preaching!

# SELECT BIBLIOGRAPHY

Achtemeier, Elizabeth. *Creative Preaching*. Abingdon, 1980.

Bartow, Charles. *God's Human Speech*. Eerdmans, 1997.

Buechner, Frederick. *Telling the Truth: The Gospel as Tragedy, Comedy & Fairy Tale*. Harper&Row, 1987.

Brueggemann, Walter. *Cadences of Home: Preaching Among Exiles*. Westminster, 1997.

Burghardt, Walter. *Preaching: The Art and the Craft*. Paulist, 1987.

_____. *Christ in Ten Thousand Places: Homilies Toward a New Millennium*. Paulist, 2000.

Buttrick, David. *Homiletic: Moves and Structures*. Fortress, 1987.

_____. *Speaking Parables: A Homiletic Guide*. Westminster/John Knox, 2000.

Carroll, Thomas K. *Preaching the Word*. Michael Glazier. 1984.

Chartier, Myron. *Preaching as Communication*. Abingdon, 1981.

Craddock, Fred. *Overhearing the Gospel*. Abingdon, 1978.

_____. *Preaching*. Abingdon, 1985.

Edwards, O.C. *Elements of Homiletic*. The Liturgical Press, 1990.

Long, Thomas. *The Witness of Preaching*. Westminster/John Knox, 1989.

Lowry, Eugene. *The Homiletical Plot*. John Knox, 1989.

_____. *The Sermon: Dancing on the Edge of Mystery*. Abingdon, 1997.

Mitchell, Henry. *Celebration and Experience in Preaching*. Abingdon, 1997.

NCCB. *Fulfilled in Your Hearing*. USCC, 1982.

Rice, Charles. *The Embodied Word*. Fortress, 1991.

_____. *Your Way With God's Word*. Cowley, 1995.

Skudlarek, William. *The Word in Worship*. Abingdon, 1981.

Thulin, Richard. *The "I" of the Sermon*. Fortress, 1989.

Troeger, Thomas. *Creating Fresh Images for Preaching*. Judson, 1982.

_____. *Imagining a Sermon*. Nashville, 1990.

Untener, Kenneth. *Preaching Better: Practical Suggestions for Homilists*. Paulist, 1999.

Van Seters, Arthur, ed. *Preaching as a Social Act*. Abingdon, 1988.

Wallace, James. *Imaginal Preaching*. Paulist, 1995.

Wilson, Paul Scott. *The Practice of Preaching*. Abingdon, 1995.

_____. *The Four Pages of the Sermon: A Guide to Biblical Preaching*. Abingdon, 1999.

# Additional Titles Published by Resurrection Press, a Catholic Book Publishing Imprint

| | |
|---|---|
| A Rachel Rosary   Larry Kupferman | $4.50 |
| Blessings All Around   Dolores Leckey | $8.95 |
| Catholic Is Wonderful   Mitch Finley | $4.95 |
| Come, Celebrate Jesus!   Francis X. Gaeta | $4.95 |
| From Holy Hour to Happy Hour   Francis X. Gaeta | $7.95 |
| Healing through the Mass   Robert DeGrandis, SSJ | $9.95 |
| The Healing Rosary   Mike D. | $5.95 |
| Healing Your Grief   Ruthann Williams, OP | $7.95 |
| Healthy and Holy Under Stress   Muto, VanKaam | $3.95 |
| Heart Peace   Adolfo Quezada | $9.95 |
| Life, Love and Laughter   Jim Vlaun | $7.95 |
| Living Each Day by the Power of Faith   Barbara Ryan | $8.95 |
| The Joy of Being a Catechist   Gloria Durka | $4.95 |
| The Joy of Being a Eucharistic Minister   Mitch Finley | $5.95 |
| The Joy of Ushers   Gretchen Hailer | $5.95 |
| Lights in the Darkness   Ave Clark, O.P. | $8.95 |
| Loving Yourself for God's Sake   Adolfo Quezada | $5.95 |
| Mother Teresa  Eugene Palumbo | $5.95 |
| Our Grounds for Hope   Fulton J. Sheen | $7.95 |
| Personally Speaking   Jim Lisante | $8.95 |
| Practicing the Prayer of Presence   van Kaam/Muto | $8.95 |
| 5-Minute Miracles   Linda Schubert | $4.95 |
| Season of New Beginnings   Mitch Finley | $4.95 |
| Season of Promises   Mitch Finley | $4.95 |
| Stay with Us   John Mullin, SJ | $3.95 |
| Surprising Mary   Mitch Finley | $7.95 |
| Teaching as Eucharist   Joanmarie Smith | $5.95 |
| What He Did for Love   Francis X. Gaeta | $5.95 |
| You Are My Beloved   Mitch Finley | $10.95 |
| Your Sacred Story   Robert Lauder | $6.95 |

For a free catalog call 1-800-892-6657